VALIANT MEN

CANADA'S VICTORIA CROSS AND GEORGE CROSS WINNERS

EDITED BY JOHN SWETTENHAM

HAKKERT / TORONTO / 1973

Canadian War Museum
Historical Publications   7

Editor: John Swettenham
Canadian War Museum,
National Museum of Man,
National Museums of Canada

Design: Helmut Rath
Composition: Joan Murray, Pam Axler, Anya Humphrey

This book has been published with the aid of funds provided by the National Museums of Canada.

© Crown Copyright 1973

Standard Book Number 88866-525-3

Library of Congress Catalogue Card Number 73-83515

A. M. Hakkert Ltd.
554 Spadina Crescent
Toronto, Canada M5S 2J9

Printed in Canada

Previous publications in the series:

[1] *Canada and the First World War*, by John Swettenham. Canadian War Museum, Ottawa, 1968.

[2] *D-Day*, by John Swettenham. Canadian War Museum, Ottawa, 1969.

[3] *Canada and the First World War*, by John Swettenham. Based on the Fiftieth Anniversary Armistice Display at the Canadian War Museum. Ryerson, Toronto, 1969. Illustrated.

[4] *Canadian Military Aircraft*, by J. A. Griffin. Queen's Printer, Ottawa, 1969.

5 *The Last War Drum: the North West Rebellion of 1885*, by Desmond Morton. Published by Hakkert, Toronto, in cooperation with the Canadian War Museum, 1972.

6 *The Evening of Chivalry*, by John Swettenham. National Museums of Canada, Ottawa, 1972.

To Canada's Victoria Cross and George Cross Winners, Past and Present

"The brave man is not he who feels no fear,
For that were stupid and irrational;
But he, whose noble soul its fear subdues,
And bravely shares the danger nature shrinks from."
      Joanna Baillie, 1762 – 1851

FOREWORD

By Admiral of the Fleet Earl Mountbatten of Burma
K.G., P.C., G.C.B., O.M., G.C.S.I., G.C.I.E., G.C.V.O., D.S.O., F.R.S.

When I was asked to write a foreword I felt greatly honoured, for this book is the first to present, in a single volume, the story of Canada's Victoria Cross and George Cross winners.

The book, let us hope, will endure as a permanent reference to an inspiring theme. It records, in chronological order, every award of either Cross to a Canadian from the Crimean War to the most recent instance. It does so with such variety, in both text and illustrations, as available sources permit; and it includes a comprehensive index. Thus we have a source of information about all these holders of the two highest Commonwealth awards — one "For Valour" regardless of rank, the other "For Gallantry" whether on the part of servicemen or civilians.

The Crosses were won in many parts of the world and in a wide variety of circumstances. The only common element was courage of an uncommon order as is expressed in the title, "Valiant Men."

Nothing I could say can add to the exploits of these men: they speak for themselves.

Mountbatten of Burma
A.F.

CONTENTS

Foreword	vii
Preface	x
Introduction	xii
Part I — Victoria Cross Winners	
The Crimean War	2
The Indian Mutiny	6
The Burma Campaign	12
The South African War	16
The First World War	26
The Second World War	166
Part II — George Cross Winners	200
Part III — Victoria Cross and George Cross Winners Associated with Canada	221
Index	229

PREFACE

With the announcement in 1972 of distinctively Canadian decorations for bravery available to civilians and servicemen of all ranks — the Cross of Valour, the Star of Courage, and the Medal of Bravery — it is timely to review the Victoria Cross and George Cross story as it relates to Canada.

The purpose of this book is to name all Canada's Victoria Cross and George Cross winners; to present them between the covers of one volume; to correct, as far as possible, previously published biographical data relating to them; and to provide the best available pictures, either of the circumstances under which the decoration was won or of the holder.

Our list of Canadian V.Cs. differs from those already published. In a country such as Canada, where immigrants come and go, this is to be expected. Thomas O. L. Wilkinson, for example, is generally listed as a Canadian V.C., yet he was born in England in 1894 and spent less than two years in Canada before the First World War. When war broke out he did not join a Canadian unit; instead, he returned to England and enlisted in a British regiment and won the V.C. while serving with it. The British, not unnaturally, claim Wilkinson as one of their own V.Cs., and we consider it right to list him merely as a V.C. winner *associated* with Canada by virtue of his short residence in this country.

Erratum:

Page x, par. 3, 3rd sentence, should read:

When war broke out, although he joined a Canadian unit, he was commissioned in the British Army as early as December 1914 and won the V. C. while serving with it.

The biographical research has been done on our behalf by Major Richard K. Malott, C.D., of Canadian Forces Headquarters, Ottawa. His work is gratefully acknowledged. Major Malott has been in touch with relatives and friends, mayors of cities and other dignitaries, the clergy and keepers of parish records. Hundreds of letters — literally — have been written. Even so, he admits, the records are often confusing and he would be grateful if any person who has evidence pointing to facts other than as stated would write to the Canadian War Museum. An example of his difficulties may be cited. The spelling of the name of Corporal Joseph Kaeble, who won the V.C. in August, 1918, is contested by the historian of his regiment, who states that the name should be Keable. There are, in fact, eight variations in the spelling of this name and though members of the family now spell the name "Keable," Joseph clearly signed his attestation papers "Kaeble," and this is how his name appears in the *London Gazette*, the records of Buckingham Palace and the Book of Remembrance. The same name — approved by his next-of-kin — is on his grave marker as well as in the records of the Commonwealth War Graves Commission. With that in mind, this gallant N.C.O. enters the book as Joseph Kaeble. Despite conflicting evidence, much new data have been established, now incorporated, and there has been a valuable by-product of Major Malott's work — three V.Cs. and one G.C. presented to the Museum. These decorations, therefore, have become part of Canada's heritage; there is no danger of them leaving this country.

Special thanks are due to Mr. Fred Gaffen who did the historical and pictorial research; he has selected accounts and illustrations which best portray these stirring actions. Mr. Frank McGuire checked the text and his work is particularly acknowledged. To these names are added those of Miss Maureen Higgs and Mr. Fred Azar, for their accurate typing of the draft, compilation of material and preparation of the index.

We are also grateful to Miss M.F.J. Dignard of the Canadian Forces Records Centre, Mr. G. N. Anderson, Head of the National Museums Photographic Section, and to the staffs of the Department of National Defence Library and the Library of Parliament for their constant help.

The book has been edited by John A. Swettenham, Curator of Historical Resources at the Museum, who is also responsible for the concept, the connecting narrative and the captions.

J. A. S.

Notes

For smoother reading, only a brief note is given with each account of a V. C. or G. C. winning exploit. The scholarly reader will find the source of quotations more fully indicated in the index under the appropriate entry. Photo and illustration acknowledgements are also more fully indicated in the index.

INTRODUCTION

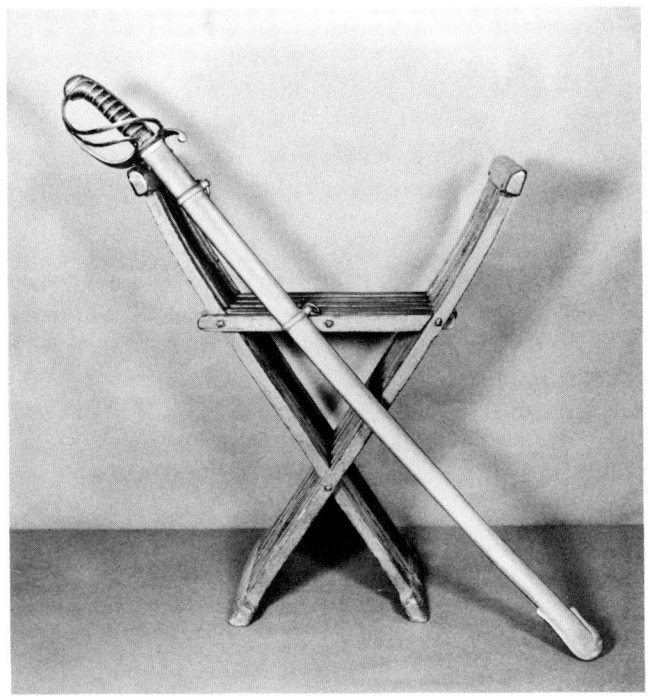

Dunn's Sword, Canadian War Museum.

The Commonwealth's highest military decoration for bravery is the Victoria Cross. It was founded by Queen Victoria in 1856 to reward outstanding gallantry in the Crimean War. The decoration, a bronze cross pattée with, in relief, the Royal crest, bears the simple words: "For Valour." It is suspended from a ribbon that was formerly blue for the navy and red for the army; the ribbon is now red (a dull crimson) for all three services.

Since a Canadian, Lieutenant Dunn, won the V.C. in "The Charge of the Light Brigade" at the Crimean battle of Balaclava, ninety-three Canadians or foreign nationals serving in Canadian units have received the award, sixty-nine of them in the First World War. Some were regulars, the majority wartime volunteers. They were of low or high rank and represent many branches of the armed forces. All were supremely brave, and that — not rank or length of service — was the sole criterion. The first posthumous V.C. was awarded in 1902 and after that there were many who never knew that their self-sacrifice had been recognized. In such cases the decoration was presented to the next-of-kin.

Though the action leading to the award must generally have been performed "in the presence of the enemy," there are exceptions. One is Private O'Hea, a British soldier, who won the only V.C. ever awarded for service in Canada when he suppressed a fire in a railway car containing live ammunition at Quebec in 1866. Another is Assistant-Surgeon Douglas, a Canadian serving with the British during the Burma campaign of 1867, who braved a raging sea to rescue soldiers who had been stranded on an island.

The V.C. cannot be awarded to civilians unless they are serving with the armed forces. During the air raids on Britain early in the Second World War, it became clear that any civilian could be brave enough to qualify for a decoration during conditions of modern warfare. Accordingly, in 1940, King George VI instituted the George Cross for civilians and members of the services alike, male or female, who performed "acts of the greatest heroism or of the most conspicuous courage in circumstances of extreme danger." This decoration — the second highest Commonwealth award for bravery — is a plain silver cross bearing in the centre a representation of Saint George slaying the dragon and the words: "For Gallantry." The ribbon is garter blue. Eight Canadians, and a Bermudian serving in a Canadian unit, have won the G.C. Not all were members of the armed forces.

Those who won these decorations deserved the distinction: the supporting evidence is too thoroughly checked for it to be otherwise. Conversely, it is undoubtedly true that many other Canadians have performed comparable acts but these lacked witnesses.

The winners, whose deeds are described, had one thing in common — courage of the highest order — and courage is not easy to define. Perhaps the American Civil War leader, General Sherman, succeeded best when he wrote:

I would define true courage to be a perfect sensibility of the measure of danger, and a mental willingness to incur it.

In all these men, when they saw what had to be done, there was a sort of obstinacy — a forcing of the will to stifle fear and a refusal to compromise in any way, even with death.

Therein lies the measure of "true courage," a theme that is consistent throughout this book.

PART I

VICTORIA CROSS WINNERS

THE CRIMEAN WAR

Balaclava, by Augustus Butler
Army Museums Ogilby Trust (London)

DUNN, Alexander Roberts

V.C.	Balaclava, October 25th, 1854
Born	York, Upper Canada, September 15th, 1833
Unit	11th (Prince Albert's Own) Regiment of (Light) Dragoons (Hussars), (British Army)
Died	Senafe, Abyssinia, January 25th, 1868

[During the Charge of the Light Brigade at Balaclava,] Lieutenant Alexander Dunn ... one of the handsomest men of his day, and also ... one of the finest swordsmen and horsemen in the Army, won the Victoria Cross; having emptied his revolver at the Russians he flung it at them and resorted to his sabre, which he used to such good effect (Dunn stood six feet three and used a sword much longer than regulations permitted) that he saved Sergeant Bentley's life by cutting down several Russians who were attacking him.

The 11th Hussars

[He then saved another life by] cutting down a Russian Hussar, who was attacking Private Levett, 11th Hussars.

London Gazette, February 24, 1857

Alexander Roberts Dunn

THE INDIAN MUTINY

The Storming of Delhi (Artist unknown)
National Army Museum

READE, Herbert Taylor

V.C.	Delhi, India, September 14th, 1857
Born	Perth, Upper Canada, September 2nd, 1828
Service	61st (South Gloucestershire) Regiment of Foot, (British Army)
Died	Bath, England, June 23rd, 1897

[During the Indian Mutiny, Surgeon Reade] ministering to the wounded up and down [the] tortuous alleys of Delhi, ... was never far from the rebels.

He ... was tending the wounds of a number of men when a large party of mutineers ... levelled a murderous fire on the men below. ...

He shouted for volunteers and a party of about ten men ... followed him. ...

The young Canadian pursued and cut down the enemy. ... Of the leader and his ten, only three returned whole. ...

But this was only one act of bravery. ... The mutineers had mounted several cannon. ... Leading his entire regiment, Reade dashed for these batteries, and a sanguinary melee ensued.

Reade fought bitterly around the guns. With a Sergeant ... he spiked one, a feat which won him the plaudits of all who had followed this intrepid fighting surgeon.

With the fall of the Magazine the way was now cleared for the complete occupation of Delhi.

"Canada's Second Victoria Cross"

Herbert Taylor Reade
Sketch by Helmut Rath from a newspaper photograph

HALL, William

V.C.	Lucknow, India, November 16th, 1857
Born	Horton Bluff, Nova Scotia, April 28th, 1827
Unit	Royal Navy (H.M.S. *Shannon*), Naval Brigade
Died	Avonport, N.S., August 25th, 1904

[The Shah Najaf, a large and ancient mosque, was the key to Lucknow, then held by Indian mutineers.]

The turning point of the battle had been reached. Either the Shah Najaf must be taken or Sir Colin Campbell's force must recoil in defeat.

Captain Peel ordered two of his guns still nearer to the mosque.... With one of these guns went William Hall.

A fire of musketry and hand grenades drenched the crews, all but annihilating them.... Calmly Hall worked [his] gun beneath that murderous storm. Only his officer ... and he were left; but with no thought beyond accomplishing what he had been ordered to do, the Nova Scotian Negro continued sponging and loading, sending shell after shell crashing into the wall....

The capture of the Shah Najaf was effected when a fissure was discovered [and] a number of Highlanders made their entry....

Both Hall and his officer were awarded the Victoria Cross for their unparalleled bravery before the walls.

"Man of Valour"

William Hall

THE BURMA CAMPAIGN

DOUGLAS, Campbell Mellis

V.C.	Island of Little Andaman, May 7th, 1867
Born	Quebec City, August 5th, 1840
Unit	24th (2nd Warwickshire) Regiment of Foot, (British Army)
Died	Wells, Somerset, December 31st, 1909

One of our ships, the *Assam Valley*, had put in at the island of Little Andaman, in the Bay of Bengal, and some of the crew went ashore. Apparently they must have been set upon and murdered by the natives, for none of them ever returned. To ascertain their fate, a party of the 24th Regiment was sent by steamer from Rangoon, and on some of them landing on May 7, 1867, they were attacked by the natives. Meantime, a storm arose and turned the surf into a raging sea, and the soldiers on the shore being in great peril, Dr. [Assistant-Surgeon] Douglas and four men most gallantly manned a gig and attempted to reach them. They very nearly succeeded in their endeavours, but the boat beginning to fill rapidly, they were forced to retire. They then made a second attempt and were successful in reaching the shore, taking off five men. On these being placed safely on board, the doctor and his four brave men turned once more to the rescue of the rest of the soldiers, and by their strenuous efforts the entire party was eventually taken off the island.

History of the Victoria Cross

Campbell Mellis Douglas

THE SOUTH AFRICAN WAR

"The Boers Rushing the British Guns"

RICHARDSON, Arthur Herbert Lindsay

V.C.	Wolve Spruit, Standerton, July 5th, 1900
Born	Southport, near Liverpool, England, 1873
Unit	Strathcona's Horse
Died	Liverpool, December 15th, 1932

On the 5th of July at Wolve Spruit one of the most daring feats of the war was performed by Sergeant A. H. L. Richardson.

Alex. Mcarthur was wounded at close range, shot in the arm and thigh; his companions had been forced to retire. In his attempt to escape his horse was shot and fell upon him, Sergeant Richardson saw his plight, and although his horse was wounded and he himself had just risen from a sick-bed, gallantly rode back under a terrific cross-fire till within 300 yards of the Boers and rescued his wounded comrade.

Canada's Sons on Kopje and Veldt

Arthur Herbert Lindsay Richardson

COCKBURN, Hampden Zane Churchill

V.C.	Leliefontein, Komati River, November 7th, 1900
Born	Toronto, November 19th, 1867
Unit	The Royal Canadian Dragoons
Died	Toronto, July 13th, 1913

Lieut. Cockburn, Lieut. Turner and Sergt. Holland won the Victoria Cross in a very gallant defence of the guns at Komati River. General Smith-Dorrien, by a wide turning movement, compelled the enemy to vacate a very strong position. The Boers were very strongly reinforced during the night and tried to recover their position next day; but Colonel Evans, with the Canadian Mounted Rifles and two guns of the 84th Battery, forestalled them, after a gallop of two miles. On the returning march, the rearguard consisted of the Canadian Dragoons and two Canadian 12-pounders, under Colonel Lessard. After some heavy fighting they were unexpectedly charged in the afternoon by 200 mounted Boers, who got within seventy yards before they were stopped by the Canadian Dragoons. Lieut. Cockburn held them off at a most critical moment and deliberately sacrificed himself and his party to let the guns get away. He was slightly wounded himself, and his men were all either killed, wounded, or taken prisoners. Later in the day Lieut. Turner, who had already been twice wounded, dismounted, and deploying his men at close quarters, drove off the enemy. Sergt. Holland worked a Colt gun with most deadly effect, until at last he found the enemy almost on top of him, and the horse attached to the carriage much blown. He then lifted the gun off the carriage, mounted his horse, and rode away with the gun under his arm.

The Victoria Cross

"Liliefontein Gun," Canadian War Museum

Then things began to happen
About 200 mounted Boers
charged down on our rear
guard shooting wildly from
horseback - in an effort to
capture our two guns -

In the mean time I had
picked up a bullet in my
left arm - but used this
as an example to the men
to rally -

As we fell back - I dismounted
the handful with me about
a dozen men - and just
then got another bullet
through my neck - And
horse was twice wounded

TURNER, Richard Ernest William

V.C.	Leliefontein, Komati River, November 7th, 1900
Born	Quebec City, July 25th, 1871
Unit	The Royal Canadian Dragoons
Died	Quebec City, June 19th, 1961

> The guns were in grave danger of being captured. Lieutenant Turner galloped up and shouted, "Dismount and hold back the enemy!" I remember him distinctly saying "Never let it be said the Canadians had let their guns be taken!" ... Again Lieutenant Turner galloped up, now seriously wounded in the neck and his arm shattered.... But the important thing was, the guns of D battery had not been captured; they had been saved by the stubborn resistance of the R.C.D.
>
> Trooper A. E. Hilder, R.C.D.

Extract from Turner's Diary

The Duke of Cornwall (later King George V), accompanied by Governor General the Earl of Minto, presents the V.C. to Turner on the Plains of Abraham, in pouring rain.

Numb. 27307.

The London Gazette.

Published by Authority.

TUESDAY, APRIL 23, 1901.

War Office, April 23, 1901.

THE King has been graciously pleased to signify His intention to confer the decoration of the Victoria Cross on the undermentioned Officers and Non-Commissioned Officer, whose claims have been submitted for His Majesty's approval, for their conspicuous bravery during the action at Komati River on the 7th November, 1900, as stated against their names :—

Regiment.	Name.	Act of Courage for which recommended.
Royal Canadian Dragoons	Lieutenant H. Z. C. Cockburn	Lieutenant Cockburn, with a handful of men, at a most critical moment held off the Boers to allow the guns to get away; to do so he had to sacrifice himself and his party, all of whom were killed, wounded, or taken prisoners, he himself being slightly wounded.
Royal Canadian Dragoons	Lieutenant R. E. W. Turner	Later in the day when the Boers again seriously threatened to capture the guns, Lieutenant Turner, although twice previously wounded, dismounted and deployed his men at close quarters and drove off the Boers, thus saving the guns.
Royal Canadian Dragoons	Sergeant E. Holland	Sergeant Holland did splendid work with his Colt gun, and kept the Boers off the two 12-pounders by its fire at close range. When he saw the enemy were too near for him to escape with the carriage, as the horse was blown, he calmly lifted the gun off and galloped away with it under his arm.

HOLLAND, Edward James Gibson

V.C.	Leliefontein, Komati River, November 7th, 1900
Born	Ottawa, February 2nd, 1878
Unit	The Royal Canadian Dragoons
Died	Cobalt, Ontario, June 18th, 1948

On the left, Sergt. Eddie Holland in charge of the Colt Machine Gun, had successfully held back the enemy, but his ammunition playing out, he finally removed the barrel from the gun ... and holding the barrel which was still hot ... I saw him gallop off to safety.

Trooper A. E. Hilder, R.C.D.

Though the Colt carriage was captured, Sergt. Holland pluckily saved the gun by taking it off and riding away with it when the Boer charge was almost up to him. Then a funny thing happened. The Boers thought they had captured the gun and tried to turn it.... When they found the gun was gone they were so angry they burned the carriage.

Lt. R. E. W. Turner, R.C.D.

THE FIRST WORLD WAR

From *Vimy*, by "Snaffles" (Charles Payne), lithograph at the Canadian War Museum

The Village Constable Greets O'Leary   **The incident that gained Michael O'Leary his V.C.**   **Two of the Villagers Looking at his Decoration**

Sergeant Michael O'Leary, who was received by the King last week and decorated with the Victoria Cross he so gallantly won at Quinchy on February 1, is spending his leave at home near Inchigeelagh, near Macroom, co. Cork, with his parents

O'LEARY, Michael

V.C.	Cuinchy, France, February 1st, 1915
Born	Macroom, Ireland, September 29th, 1889
Unit	1st Battalion, The Irish Guards (British Army)
Died	London, England, August 2nd, 1961

On the last day of January the Germans attempted a surprise against the trenches neighbouring those of the Irish Guards. The position was lost, and had to be retaken.... The morning ... broke fine and clear, and simultaneously a storm of shot and shell descended on the German trenches which were marked down for recapture.... O'Leary ... marked down the spot where a German machine gun was to be found ... and it was a matter of life and death to perhaps hundreds of his comrades that he should reach it in time to prevent its being brought into action. He put on his best pace, and within a few seconds found himself in a corner of the German trench on the way to his goal. Immediately ahead of him was a barricade ... but to O'Leary ... it was no obstacle, and its five defenders quickly paid with their lives.... Leaving his five victims, O'Leary started off to cover the eighty yards that still separated him from the second barricade, where the German machine gun was hidden. He was literally now racing with death.... At every moment he expected to hear the sharp burr of the gun in action. A patch of boggy ground prevented a direct approach to the barricade, and it was with veritable anguish that he realized the necessity of a detour by a railway line.... A few seconds passed, and then, the Germans working feverishly to remount their machine gun and bring it into action, ... perceived ... O'Leary, a few yards on their right with his rifle levelled at them. The officer in charge had no time to realize that his finger was on the button before death squared his account. Two other reports followed in quick succession, and two other figures fell to the ground with barely a sound. The two survivors ... threw up their hands. With his two captives before him, the gallant Irishman returned in triumph, while his comrades swept the enemy out of the trenches, and completed one of the most successful local actions we have ever undertaken.

The Victoria Cross

FISHER, Fred

V.C.	St. Julien, Belgium, April 23rd, 1915 (Posthumous)
Born	St. Catharines, Ontario, August 3rd, 1894
Unit	13th Battalion, Canadian Expeditionary Force
Died	April 23rd, 1915

No account of the 13th Battalion in the Second Battle of Ypres is complete without reference to the work of this plucky N.C.O.... Coming forward from St. Julien, Fisher discovered that some [Canadian] guns ... were being fought with the German infantry close on top of them. Capture of these guns seemed imminent, but Fisher set up his machine gun in advance of the Battery, and ... held off the enemy till the guns got away.... During this encounter Fisher's small section was under concentrated fire and four of his six men were killed. Returning to St. Julien, he got four men ... and endeavoured once more to push up to the front line. In coming forward he lost these men and eventually reached the front line alone. Here he continued to render valuable service up to the moment of his death.

The 13th Battalion Royal Highlanders of Canada

Fred Fisher
Painting by George J. Coates. Canadian War Museum

HALL, Frederick William

V.C.	Ypres, Belgium, April 24th, 1915 (Posthumous)
Born	Kilkenny, Ireland, February 21st, 1885
Unit	8th Battalion, C.E.F.
Died	April 24th, 1915

In moving up to our fire-trench the . . . troops had to cross a high bank which was fully exposed to the rifle and machine gun fire of the enemy. . . . Its crest was continuously swept by bullets . . . and the incoming battalion suffered a number of casualties. . . . Sergeant-Major Hall missed a member of his company on two separate occasions and . . . left the trench and went back to the top of the bank, under cover of the dark, returning each time with a wounded man. At nine o'clock in the morning of the 24th, the attention of the occupants of the trench was attracted to the top of the bank by groans. . . . Hall immediately suggested a rescue . . . and Corporal Payne and Private Rogerson as promptly volunteered to accompany him. The three went over the parados . . . and instantly drew a heavy fire . . . both Payne and Rogerson were wounded. They crawled and scrambled back to the shelter of the trench, with Hall's assistance. There the Sergeant-Major rested for a few minutes, before attempting the rescue again. He refused to be accompanied the second time. . . . The fire from the hostile positions in front and on the flanks of this point in our line was now hot and accurate. It was deliberate, aimed fire, discharged in broad daylight over adjusted sights at an expected target. Hall knew all this, but he crawled out of the trench. . . . Very low shots, ricocheting off the top of the parados . . . whined and hummed in erratic flight. He reached . . . the slope of the bank without being hit . . . and joined the wounded man. . . . He lay flat and squirmed himself beneath the other's helpless body. Thus he got the sufferer on his back, in position to be moved; but in the act of raising his head slightly to glance over the way by which he must regain the shelter of the trench, he received a bullet in the brain.

Thirty Canadian V.Cs.

"The Rescue"

BELLEW, Edward Donald

V.C.	Near Keerselaere, Belgium, April 24th, 1915
Born	Bombay, India, October 28th, 1882
Unit	7th Battalion, C.E.F.
Died	Kamloops, B.C., February 1st, 1961

During the German attack on the Ypres salient, Capt. (then Lieut.) Bellew, as Battalion Machine Gun Officer, had two guns in action on the high ground overlooking Keerselaere. The enemy's attack broke in full force on the morning of the 24th against the front and right flank of the Battalion — the latter being exposed owing to a gap in the line. The right Company was soon put out of action, but the advance was temporarily stayed by Capt. Bellew, who had sited his guns on the left of the right Company. Reinforcements were sent forward but they in turn were surrounded and destroyed. With the enemy in strength less than 100 yards from him, with no further assistance in sight, and with his rear threatened, Capt. Bellew and Sergt. Peerless, each operating a gun, decided to stay where they were and fight it out. Sergt. Peerless was killed and Capt. Bellew was wounded and fell. Nevertheless, he got up and maintained his fire till ammunition failed and the enemy rushed the position. Capt. Bellew then seized a rifle, smashed his machine gun, and fighting to the last, was taken prisoner.

London Gazette, May 15, 1919

[He was a prisoner of war until the early part of 1919 and it was not before his return to Vancouver that the award was announced.]

From "The Battle of Second Ypres," by W. B. Wollen

SCRIMGER, Francis Alexander Caron

V.C.	Ypres, April 25th, 1915
Born	Montreal, February 10th, 1881
Service	Canadian Army Medical Corps (Attached to 14th Battalion, C.E.F.)
Died	Montreal, February 13th, 1937

[During the Second Battle of Ypres Captain Scrimger] was in charge of an advanced dressing station situated in an old farm building near the battered city of Ypres. The house was surrounded by a moat over which there was only one road. . . .

On the afternoon of the 25th the German artillery sent over incendiary shells, and one of these, landing on the farm, set the place alight. . . .

The single road was almost impassable owing to a heavy German shrapnel barrage. . . . Some of the staff, and some of the less badly wounded patients, swam the moat. They were all removed except one badly injured officer; for him swimming was out of the question.

Scrimger took upon himself the task of saving this patient . . . protecting him with his body as the splinters fell around them, and finally, during a lull, carried him out of the blazing house on his back. . . . There was no shelter in sight. . . .

Laying his patient down, Scrimger remained beside him, shielding him again with his own body, till help arrived later in the day.

Thirty Canadian V.Cs.

Captain Scrimger carried me . . . to a moat . . . where we lay half under water. . . . [He] curled his body round my head and shoulders to protect me. We were there under heavy shell fire all the time.

The Canadian Gazette, July 22, 1915
quoting Capt. H. F. McDonald

"A First-Aid Dressing Station Under Fire"

CAMPBELL, Frederick William

V.C.	Givenchy, France, June 15th, 1915 (Posthumous)
Born	Mount Forest, Ontario, June 15th, 1867
Unit	1st Battalion, C.E.F.
Died	June 19th, 1915

With the second wave of the attack came Lieutenant Campbell, his two Colt machine-guns and their crews. On the way, before reaching the shelter of the captured trench, all the members of one of his gun-crews were wiped out. He got into the trench with only one of his guns and a few unwounded men. He immediately moved to the left towards Stony Mountain, until he was halted by a block in the trench. By this time one Private Vincent was the only man of his two crews still standing and unhit. All the others lay dead or wounded behind him. Vincent, who had been a lumberjack in the woods of Ontario in the days of peace, was as strong of body as of heart and a cool hand into the bargain. When his officer failed to find a suitable base for his gun in that particular position, Vincent saved time by offering his own broad back. So Campbell straddled Vincent's back with the tripod of the gun and opened fire on the enemy.

By this time our supply of bombs had given out and our attack was weakening. The Germans massed for a counter-attack. Campbell fired over a thousand rounds from his gun, from Vincent's back, dispersed the enemy's initial counter-attack, and afterwards maintained his position until the trench was entered by German bombers and he was seriously wounded. Then Vincent abandoned the tripod and dragged the gun away to safety.

Campbell crawled back towards his friends. He was met and lifted by Sergeant-Major Owen and carried into our jumping-off trench. [He died four days later.]

Thirty Canadian V.Cs.

Artist's impression

CLARKE, Leo

V.C.	Pozières, France, September 9th, 1916
Born	Waterdown, Ontario, December 1st, 1892
Unit	2nd Battalion, C.E.F.
Died	October 19th, 1916

[During the Battles of the Somme] a fiery hurricane ... swept Pozières Ridge. [Corporal Clarke was consolidating a newly captured trench when two officers, with about twenty of the enemy, counter-attacked. Clarke] advanced ... to meet the Germans.... The corporal emptied his revolver into them, refilled and emptied it a second time.... Then picking up a German rifle ... he fired the undischarged cartridges.

But the enemy were now on him. One of the officers ... made a lunge at the corporal, wounding him in the knee. Clarke shot him dead.... Bleeding profusely, the indomitable youth carried the battle to the Germans once more. However, they had had enough. Turning tail, they fled, and as they scrambled wildly in a panic-stricken mob, Clarke picked them off and pursued them until only one was left.

The History of the 2nd Canadian Battalion
(Eastern Ontario Regiment)

[During this war, for the first time in Canada, Clarke's V.C. was presented by the Governor General. The Duke of Devonshire handed the decoration to Clarke's representative at a ceremony attended by about 30,000 people.]

Times History of the War, vol. xii

Leo Clarke

KERR, John Chipman

V.C.	Courcelette, France, September 16th, 1916
Born	Fox River, Nova Scotia, January 11th, 1887
Unit	49th Battalion, C.E.F.
Died	Port Moody, B.C., February 19th, 1963

[Kerr] advanced about thirty yards into the hostile position before a sentry took alarm and hurled a grenade. [He] saw the grenade coming and ... attempted to protect himself with his arm. He was partially successful ... for ... the bomb ... did no more than blow off the upper joint of his right fore-finger and wound him slightly in the right side.

The exchange of bombs between the defenders and attackers now became general. ... Good throwing was done by our men ... but Kerr felt that the affair promised to settle into a stationary action unless something new and sudden happened. So he clambered out of the trench ... and moved along the parados until he came into close contact with, and full view of, the enemy. ... Despite loss of blood, he was still full of enterprise and fight. He tossed [his] grenades among the crowded defenders beneath him and then opened fire into them with his rifle. ...

While Kerr pumped lead into the massed enemy beneath his feet he directed the fire of his bombers so effectively, by voice and gesture, that the defenders were forced back to the shelter of the nearest bay. He immediately jumped down into the trench and went after them, with all the Canadian bombers and bayonet-men at his heels. A dug-out was reached ... Kerr went on alone, rounded a bay and once again joined battle with the defenders of the trench. But the spirit of combat, even of resistance, had gone out of them. Up went their hands!

Before having his wounds dressed, Private Kerr escorted the 62 Germans across open ground, under heavy fire, to a support trench.

Thirty Canadian V.Cs.

Bombers on the Western Front

RICHARDSON, James Cleland

V.C.	The Somme, France, October 8th, 1916 (Posthumous)
Born	Bellshill, Lanark, Scotland, November 25th, 1895
Unit	16th Battalion, C.E.F.
Died	October 8th, 1916

The situation on the centre and left of the Battalion front, where the wire was totally uncut, at the time Richardson started to play was desperately critical. Not a 16th man had got over the wire. . . . It seemed as if the attacking troops to a man would become casualties.

Richardson, at this moment, took the lead and according to the evidence of different men, played up and down in front of the wire for fully ten minutes.

Piper Richardson was only eighteen years old. He was not originally detailed for the attack. He asked to be paraded before the Commanding Officer; and there pleaded so earnestly to be allowed to go into action, that Colonel Leckie finally granted him his wish.

[A Company Sergeant-Major reported:] Piper Jimmy Richardson came over to me at this moment and asked if he could help, but I told him our company commander was gone. Things looked very bad and then it was that the piper asked if he could play his pipes – "Wull I gie them wund (wind)?" was what he said. I told him to go ahead and as soon as he got them going I got what men I could together, we got through the wire.

The History of the 16th Battalion

Piper Richardson

HARVEY, Frederick Maurice Watson

V.C.	Guyencourt, France, March 27th, 1917
Born	Athboy, County Meath, Ireland, September 1st, 1888
Unit	Lord Strathcona's Horse (Royal Canadians), C.E.F.

Residing at Calgary, Alberta

The Strathconas, with Guyencourt in view, charged on to a ridge . . . where they were confronted by machine guns and strongly-wired positions; so they swung to the right, rode at the north-west corner of the village and won to the partial shelter of its walls. It was at this stage of the swift action that Lieut. Harvey performed the conspicuous deed of valour that was recognized by the highest award. He commanded the leading troop of the charging Strathconas and rode well in front of his men. He was close to the edge of the village, when, by the failing light, he discovered a deadly menace to his command set fairly across his course — a wired trench containing a machine gun and a strong garrison. He swung from his saddle and sprinted straight at the gun, firing his revolver as he ran. He reached the triple entanglement and hurdled it, shot the machine gunner and jumped on to the gun. . . . Thus the trench became ours, the Strathconas took Guyencourt, and Harvey won the Cross.

The Victoria Cross

The Investiture by King George V

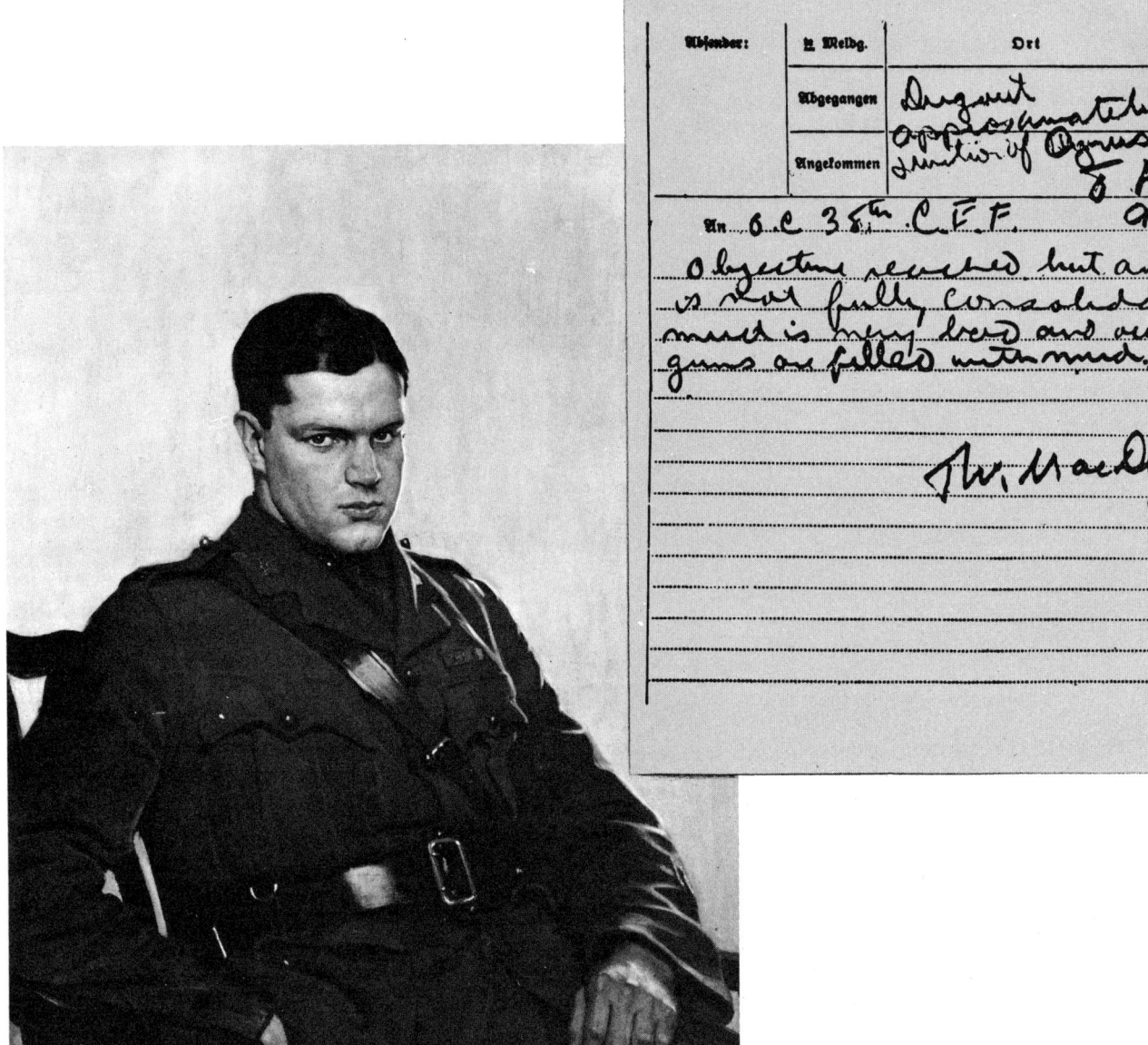

MacDOWELL, Thain Wendell

V.C.	Vimy Ridge, France, April 9th, 1917
Born	Lachute, Quebec, September 16th, 1890
Unit	38th Battalion, C.E.F.
Died	Nassau, Bahamas, March 29th, 1960

[During the Battle of Vimy Ridge, Captain MacDowell] found himself alone with two runners. The German dug-out where he aimed at establishing himself could be seen in the shell-torn line, but there was no time to collect a party to clean the place up. But on the way to his destination MacDowell captured two enemy machine guns as an aside. He bombed one out of action, then attacked the other. The second gunner did not wait but ran for shelter to a dug-out whither MacDowell followed and got him.

Working their way along to the big dug-out the three Canadians saw that the place was more formidable than they had anticipated. . . . MacDowell bawled down the deep passage, summoning the German occupants to surrender. No answer came. . . . The captain decided to go down. . . .

Suddenly, as he turned a corner, which led into the main room of this subterranean fortress, he found himself face to face with a large group of the enemy. There were seventy-seven of them. . . .

Quick as a flash he turned and began to shout orders to an imaginary force behind him — and up went the hands of the seventy-seven stalwart [Prussian] Guards.

Thirty Canadian V.Cs.

Thain Wendell MacDowell
Painting by Harold Knight. Canadian War Museum

MILNE, William Johnstone

V.C.	Vimy Ridge, April 9th, 1917 (Posthumous)
Born	Wishaw, Scotland, December 21st, 1892
Unit	16th Battalion, C.E.F.
Died	April 9th, 1917

[On the front of the 16th Battalion, during the Battle of Vimy Ridge] a German machine gun opened fire ... inflicting many casualties. ... Groups crept towards it from three sides but with no effect. ... A series of bomb explosions was heard in the direction of the enemy gun and ... Private Milne sprang up from a shell-hole close to it, signalling to his comrades to advance. He had crawled round on his hands and knees to within bombing distance of the enemy machine gun crew, and with hand grenades had put every one of them out of action. Later in the attack ... Milne ... put out of action another German machine gun which was seriously holding up the advance. ... Milne was killed before the day's fighting closed.

History of the 16th Battalion

Storming Vimy Ridge

SIFTON, Ellis Wellwood

V.C.	Vimy Ridge, April 9th, 1917 (Posthumous)
Born	Wallacetown, Ontario, October 12th, 1891
Unit	18th Battalion, C.E.F.
Died	April 9th, 1917

[On Vimy Ridge] the first German line was gained and captured.... But at the second line, after the barrage had swept over it, the first opposition of importance was met. Here small parties of machine gunners, tucked away in their concrete fortresses, had escaped the terrible shelling and as the Canadians advanced they enfiladed the waves of men as they passed.

One such nest stemmed the advance of 'C' Company. Men began to fall, hit by the unseen enemy. The others peered around in the gloom, trying to discover the nest. Lance-Sergeant Sifton saw it first. The barrel of the gun showed over a parapet.

Sifton did not wait to work out an elaborate attack, for there was no time to lose. He rushed ahead, leaped into the trench, charged into the crew, overthrew the gun and turned on the gunners with his bayonet. Before they had time to resist, every one of the Germans was out of business. With the demolition of the machine gun, the advance of the 18th Battalion moved on.

Sifton's men hurried up to support him, but before they reached the position a party of Germans advanced on him from down the trench. He attacked them with bayonet and clubbed rifle and held them off till his comrades jumped into the trench and ended the unequal fight. But none noticed a dying German, one of Sifton's victims, who rolled over to the edge of the trench, picked up a rifle and took careful aim....

Thirty Canadian V.Cs.

Ellis Wellwood Sifton

PATTISON, John George

V.C.	Vimy Ridge, April 10th, 1917
Born	Woolwich, England, September 8th, 1875
Unit	50th Battalion, C.E.F.
Died	June 3rd, 1917

[Sometimes, as at Vimy, a company finds itself held] before an embattled fortification whose point of vantage covers the whole local zone of attack.... On that April afternoon the 50th Battn. encountered just such a check.... Each time they had been beaten back with heavy losses.... Another attack was organized, with no more success than the last; and then, as so often occurs, a critical situation was relieved by the clearheaded bravery of a single soldier. Private Pattison, an engineer from Calgary, proceeded to deal with the situation. He advanced single-handed towards the machine gun post in a series of short rapid dashes, taking cover on the way in available shell-holes while deciding his next point of vantage. In a few moments he had reached a shell-hole within thirty yards of the vital strong-point. He stood up in full view of the machine gunners and under their point-blank fire threw three bombs with such good aim that the guns were put out of action and the crews temporarily demoralized. This was Pattison's opportunity, and he took it without hesitation. As his last bomb exploded amidst the Germans he rushed across the intervening space, and in a moment was using his bayonet upon the ... enemy. He had killed them all before his companions had caught him up. Twenty minutes later all objectives were gained and the Canadians busy consolidating the captured line. Pattison came unscathed through the day's fighting and ... the following day; but he never wore his V.C. [He was killed in June.]

Thirty Canadian V.Cs.

"Storming a trench with bombs and bayonet"

COMBE, Robert Grierson

V.C.	Acheville, France, May 3rd, 1917 (Posthumous)
Born	Aberdeen, Scotland, August 5th, 1880
Unit	27th Battalion, C.E.F.
Died	May 3rd, 1917

They had only gone two hundred yards when the German artillery shortened range and the full force of the barrage fell on them. Under that staggering blow men collapsed in dozens, crushed by the weight of uptorn earth or blown to fragments. In the right company, Lieut. Combe was the only officer who had survived so far. His company was but a tattered remnant of what it had been a few moments before; but Combe had his orders . . . and he meant to carry them out. Collecting the handful of men left to him he began to work his way through the German barrage. He managed it. He brought his followers safely through that terrible curtain of fire, only to find that if he would reach the German line he must also get through the barrage of our own guns. He steadied his men and accomplished the second journey also . . . and he had only five men left when he reached the German trenches. . . .

Combe and his men . . . entered the German trench . . . aided by a few men of another company whom they had picked up. They bombed the Germans along the trench with German bombs, having exhausted their own long before. Eighty prisoners . . . were on their way back to our lines, and 250 yards of trench were in the hands of the invaders. Again and again the gallant little band charged the enemy, Combe always at their head, leading them around traverses and into dug-outs. Along the whole of that 250 yards of trench lay dead and dying Germans. Combe was killed by a rifle bullet as he was leading his . . . bombers up the trench in the climax of his triumph.

The Victoria Cross

Robert Grierson Combe, by R. M. Morgan

BISHOP, William Avery

V.C.	Near Cambrai, France, June 2nd, 1917
Born	Owen Sound, Ontario, February 8th, 1894
Service	Royal Flying Corps
Died	Palm Beach, Florida, September 11th, 1956

["Billy" Bishop flew with the Royal Flying Corps and was the greatest Commonwealth "ace" of the war. In all, he scored seventy-two victories over enemy aircraft. He won the Victoria Cross on June 2nd, 1917, when he crossed the enemy lines alone and attacked a German aerodrome twelve miles behind the front. Four aircraft rose to meet him but Bishop shot three down, one after the other, then emptied his Lewis gun at the fourth machine before escaping to his station.]

At the age of 24, Bishop had won almost all the coveted awards of war service. . . . His late Majesty King George personally pinned the medals on Bishop at Buckingham Palace and told him he was the only man who had received the Victoria Cross, the Military Cross and the Distinguished Service Order at the same time.

The Legionary, March, 1940

William Avery Bishop
Painting by Alphonse Jongers. Canadian War Museum

BROWN, Harry

V.C.	Hill 70 (near Lens, France), August 16th, 1917 (Posthumous)
Born	Ganonoque, Ontario, May 11th, 1898
Unit	10th Battalion, C.E.F.
Died	August 17th, 1917

[After a position had been captured by the Canadians during the stern fighting at Hill 70, the enemy delivered a massive counter-blow. A message had to be sent calling for artillery to smash the German attack.]

Then occurred one of many acts of heroism that illumine the dark pages of war. With all [signal] wires cut, communications between the 10th Battalion's company and battalion headquarters could be maintained only by runner. To ensure [the] message being delivered, two runners had to venture back through an intense barrage. One was killed; but the other, Private Harry Brown, his arm shattered, doggedly struggled through to complete his mission before collapsing unconscious on the dug-out steps. He died of his wounds.

Canadian Expeditionary Force

"The Runner's Last Stride"

O'ROURKE, Michael James

V.C.	Hill 70, August 15th – 18th, 1917
Born	Limerick, Ireland, March 19th, 1878
Unit	7th Battalion, C.E.F.
Died	December 6th, 1957

For conspicuous gallantry and devotion to duty over a prolonged period as a stretcher bearer in bringing in wounded under concentrated and accurate machine gun and rifle fire.

A Short History of the 7th Battalion

Seeing a comrade who had been blinded stumbling around ahead of our trench, in full view of the enemy who were sniping him, Pte. O'Rourke jumped out of his trench and brought the man back, being himself heavily sniped at while doing so. Again he went forward about 50 yards in front of our barrage under very heavy and accurate fire from enemy machine guns and snipers, and brought in a comrade. On a subsequent occasion, when the line of advanced posts was retired to the line to be consolidated, he went forward under very heavy enemy fire of every description and brought back a wounded man who had been left behind.

He showed throughout an absolute disregard for his own safety, going wherever there were wounded to succour.

London Gazette, November 8, 1917

Michael James O'Rourke
Painting by Ernest Fosbery. Canadian War Museum

HOBSON, Frederick

V.C.	Hill 70, August 18th, 1917 (Posthumous)
Born	London, England, September 23rd, 1875
Unit	20th Battalion, C.E.F.
Died	August 18th, 1917

[During the Hill 70 fighting] at the time of a strong counter-attack, a Lewis gun in a forward post ... was buried by a shell, and the crew killed.... [Sergeant Hobson], though not a gunner, but grasping the great importance of the post, rushed from his trench, dug out the gun and put it into action.... A "jam" caused the gun to stop firing. Though wounded, he ... rushed forward at the advancing enemy and with bayonet and clubbed rifle, single-handed held them back until he ... was killed.... When the trench was cleared it was found that 15 of the enemy dead were lying about him.

History of the Twentieth Canadian Battalion

Artist's impression

LEARMONTH, Okill Massey

V.C.	Hill 70, August 18th, 1917 (Posthumous)
Born	Quebec City, February 22nd, 1894
Service	2nd Battalion, C.E.F.
Died	August 19th, 1917

When a portion of the company recoiled from the massive assault, the Company Commander [Major Learmonth] leaped in and himself bombed the attacking Germans. . . . He was wounded as . . . he stood like some flaxen-haired Ajax defying the fires of the enemy. In spite of his wound, he remained. A second time Learmonth was hit. . . . The men saw their Company Commander, sorely stricken but still full of fight; and the spectacle inspired them. Wave after wave of the enemy launched the most violent assaults against No. 3 Company, to no purpose. . . . For a third time Major Learmonth was wounded. . . . He asked to be laid in the trench where . . . he continued to direct the resistance. . . .

The time came . . . when Learmonth could carry on no longer. Not, however, until he had turned over his command, complete in all details, to Lieut. Hugh Smith, did he consent to be carried out. On his way he insisted on being borne to Battalion Headquarters where, although it was quite apparent that he was dying, he gave to Major Vanderwater a comprehensive verbal report on the whole of the morning's operations.

History of the 2nd Canadian Battalion

Okill Massey Learmonth
Painting by James Quinn. Canadian War Museum

HANNA, Robert

V.C.	Hill 70, August 21st, 1917
Born	Kilkeel, County Down, Ireland, August 6th, 1887
Unit	29th Battalion, C.E.F.
Died	Mount Lehman, B.C., June 15th, 1967

For most conspicuous bravery in attack, when his company met with most severe enemy resistance and all the company officers became casualties. A strong point, heavily protected by wire and held by a machine gun, had beaten off three assaults of the company with heavy casualties. This Warrant Officer [Company Sergeant-Major Hanna] under heavy machine gun and rifle fire, coolly collected a party of men, and leading them against this strong point, rushed through the wire and personally bayonetted three of the enemy and brained the fourth, capturing the position and silencing the machine gun.

London Gazette, November 8, 1917

Hanna (in raincoat) shakes hands
with fellow V.C.-winner Michael James O'Rourke
after the investiture

KONOWAL, Filip

V.C.	Hill 70, August 22nd-24th, 1917
Born	Kedeski, Russia, March 25th, 1887
Unit	47th Battalion, C.E.F.
Died	Ottawa, June 3rd, 1959

For most conspicuous bravery and leadership when in charge of a section in attack. His section had the difficult task of mopping up cellars, craters and machine-gun emplacements.

London Gazette, November 26, 1917

Entering one of these houses Konowal ... dropped daringly into the cellar. Three men fired at him as he landed, but this he escaped unharmed. Then ensued a sanguinary battle in the dark, a mêlée of rifle fire and bayonets, with the odds three to one. Finally the scuffling ceased and Konowal emerged into the daylight....

There was a large crater to the east of the road, and from the bodies of our good men before the edge it seemed obvious that a German machine gun had been in position there. Halting his men, Konowal advanced alone. Upon reaching the lip of the crater he saw seven Germans endeavouring to move the ubiquitous machine gun into a dug-out. He opened fire at once, killing three, and then, charging down upon them, accounted for the rest with the bayonet....

Heavy fighting continued throughout the night, and in the morning troops of the 44th Battalion, who were making an attack ... requested the aid of a party of the 47th in a raid upon a machine-gun emplacement in a tunnel.... Corporal Konowal was an expert in this subterranean fighting, and his party succeeded in entering the tunnel. Two charges of ammonal, successfully exploded, somewhat demoralized the German garrison, and then Konowal, dashing forward in the darkness with the utter disregard of his own safety he had displayed all through the fighting, engaged the machine-gun crew with the bayonet, overcoming and killing them all.

Thirty Canadian V.Cs.

This non-commissioned officer alone killed at least sixteen of the enemy, and during the two days' actual fighting carried on continuously his good work until severely wounded.

London Gazette, November 26, 1917

Filip Konowal
Painting by Ambrose McEvoy. Canadian War Museum

BENT, Philip Eric

V.C.	Polygon Wood, Belgium, October 10th, 1917 (Posthumous)
Born	Halifax, N.S., January 3rd, 1891
Unit	The Leicestershire Regiment (British Army)
Died	October 10th, 1917

For most conspicuous bravery, when during a heavy hostile attack, the right of his command and the battalion on his right were forced back. The situation was critical owing to the confusion caused by the attack and the intense artillery fire. Lt.-Col. Bent personally collected a platoon that was in reserve, and together with men from other companies and various regimental details, he organised and led them forward to the counter-attack, after issuing orders to other officers as to the further defence of the line. The counter-attack was successful and the enemy was checked.

The coolness and magnificent example shown to all ranks by Lt.-Col. Bent resulted in the securing of a portion of the line which was of essential importance for subsequent operations.

This very gallant officer was killed whilst leading a charge which he inspired with the call of "Come on the Tigers."

London Gazette, January 11, 1918

Artist's impression

HOLMES, Thomas William

V.C.	Passchendaele, Belgium, October 26th, 1917
Born	Montreal, August 17th, 1898
Unit	4th Canadian Mounted Rifles Battalion, C.E.F.
Died	Toronto, January 4th, 1950

For most conspicuous bravery and resource when the right flank of our attack was held up by heavy machine-gun and rifle fire from a "pill-box" strong point. Heavy casualties were producing a critical situation when Pte. Holmes, on his own initiative and single-handed, ran forward and threw two bombs, killing and wounding the crews of two machine guns. He then returned to his comrades, secured another bomb, and again rushed forward alone under heavy fire and threw the bomb into the entrance of the "pill-box," causing the nineteen occupants to surrender.

By this act of valour at a very critical moment Pte. Holmes undoubtedly cleared the way for the advance of our troops and saved the lives of many of his comrades.

London Gazette, January 11, 1918

One does not know how Private Holmes escaped the sweeping fire that was poured upon him, but there is no doubt that his gallant action . . . allowed our men to push forward and establish a strong line in advance of their immediate objective.

Thirty Canadian V.Cs.

Private Holmes, V.C. (Centre)

SHANKLAND, Robert

V.C.	Passchendaele, October 26th, 1917
Born	Ayr, Scotland, October 10th, 1887
Unit	43rd Battalion, C.E.F.
Died	Vancouver, January 20th, 1968

For most conspicuous bravery and resource in action under critical and adverse conditions.

Having gained a position, he [Lieutenant Shankland] rallied the remnant of his own platoon and men of other companies, disposed them to command the ground in front, and inflicted heavy casualties upon the retreating enemy. Later he dispersed a counter-attack, thus enabling supporting troops to come up unmolested.

He then personally communicated to Battalion Headquarters an accurate and valuable report as to the position on the Brigade frontage, and after doing so rejoined his command and carried on until relieved.

His courage and splendid example inspired all ranks and coupled with his great gallantry and skill undoubtedly saved a very critical situation.

London Gazette, December 18, 1917

By coincidence three V.C. winners — Sergeant-Major F. W. Hall, Corporal Leo Clarke and Lieutenant Shankland — all lived on Pine Street, Winnipeg, which was later renamed Valour Road.

The Legionary, November, 1965.

Artist's impression

O'KELLY, Christopher Patrick John

V.C.	Passchendaele, October 26th, 1917
Born	Winnipeg, November 18th, 1895
Unit	52nd Battalion, C.E.F.
Died	Lac Seul, Ontario, November 15th, 1922

While some forty men of Lieut. Shankland's company of the 43rd had managed to fight their way to the crest of the spur [see preceding page] ... O'Kelly, in charge of A company [52nd Battalion] was ordered to move at once to their assistance.

[He] brought his men up well, and sweeping over the brow, they caught the flank of the enemy advancing against the 43rd Battn. post, driving the Germans before them and shooting them down as they ran. For a moment it was a most successful rout, but then the fire from the pill-boxes grew heavier, and there ensued a series of gallant attacks upon the strong points before them.... O'Kelly led his men with wonderful judgment, selecting the point and method of attack with cool precision, and never losing sight of this main object — to gain ground and consolidate the ridge.

The Victoria Cross

[According to the *London Gazette*, January 11, 1918:]

Capt. O'Kelly advanced his command over 1,000 yards under heavy fire without any artillery barrage, took the enemy positions on the crest of the hill by storm, and then personally organised and led a series of attacks against "pill-boxes," his company alone capturing six of them with 100 prisoners and 10 machine-guns.

Later on in the afternoon, under the leadership of this gallant officer, his company repelled a strong counter-attack, taking more prisoners, and subsequently during the night captured a hostile raiding party consisting of one officer, 10 men, and a machine-gun.

The whole of these achievements was chiefly due to the magnificent courage, daring and ability of Capt. O'Kelly.

Christopher Patrick John O'Kelly

MacKENZIE, Hugh

V.C.	Passchendaele, October 30th, 1917 (Posthumous)
Born	Liverpool, England, December 5th, 1885
Unit	7th Canadian Machine Gun Company, C.E.F.
Died	October 30th, 1917

[The Patricias' field of attack was limited by swampy ground to a narrow strip] every foot of which was exposed to the fire of the machine-guns upon the slope.

One pill-box in particular on the crest of the hill maintained such a murderous fire that the attacking company of the Princess Pats was brought to a halt upon the slope of the hill, with every officer and N.C.O. shot down, and the men remaining seeking what cover they could, unable to advance and unwilling to retreat.... Noting the hesitation of our men on the slope of the hill, [MacKenzie] left a corporal in charge of his [machine] guns, and made his way through the heavy fire to our fellows in their terribly exposed position. . . . Taking command of the company, he . . . instantly set about arranging a plan for the downfall of the pill-box above them. Not only was there the pill-box to deal with, but the upper hill was a veritable nest of machine-guns, and MacKenzie had to make a daring reconnaissance before he could effect a suitable scheme of attack.

Detailing small parties, he sent them off to work their way round the flanks . . . to be prepared . . . to make an attack from the rear upon the pill-box that was holding up the advance. Then he arranged the frontal attack, choosing himself to lead a small party of men directly up the slope to the fort, while the remainder of his men attacked the same front from a different angle. At the word they went forward, MacKenzie leading the forlorn hope on the most exposed front of the attack. It was not possible to win through such fire unharmed, and he was shot through the head and killed at the moment of the capture of the pill-box by the flanking parties he had detailed.

Thirty Canadian V.Cs.

"Pill-box fighting"

MULLIN, George Harry

V.C.	Passchendaele, October 30th, 1917
Born	Portland, Oregon, U.S.A., August 15th, 1892
Unit	Princess Patricia's Canadian Light Infantry, C.E.F.
Died	Regina, Saskatchewan, April 5th, 1963

[While machine-gun officer Hugh MacKenzie, whose gallantry has already been described, drew the German fire, Sergeant Mullin] actually performed the incredible feat of taking the pill-box single-handed. "He rushed a snipers' post in front and destroyed the garrison with bombs, and crawling on to the top of the pill-box shot the two machine gunners with his revolver. Sergeant Mullin then rushed to another entrance and compelled the garrison of ten to surrender. His gallantry and fearlessness were witnessed by many, and although rapid fire was directed upon him, and his clothes riddled by bullets, he never faltered in his purpose, and he not only helped to save the situation but also indirectly saved many lives."

Princess Patricia's Canadian Light Infantry
citing the *London Gazette*

"Tackling a pill-box"

KINROSS, Cecil John

V.C.	Passchendaele, October 30th, 1917
Born	Uxbridge, Middlesex, England, February 17th, 1896
Unit	49th Battalion, C.E.F.
Died	Lougheed, Alberta, June 21st, 1957

Shortly after the attack [on Passchendaele Ridge] was launched, the company to which he belonged came under intense artillery fire, and further advance was held up by very severe fire from an enemy machine gun. Pte. Kinross, making a careful survey of the situation, deliberately divested himself of all his equipment save his rifle and bandolier and . . . advanced alone over the open ground in broad daylight, charged the enemy machine gun, killing the crew of six, and seized and destroyed the gun. His superb example and courage instilled the greatest confidence in his company, and enabled a further advance of 300 yards to be made and a highly important position to be established.

Throughout the day he showed marvellous coolness and courage, fighting with the utmost aggressiveness against heavy odds until seriously wounded.

London Gazette, January 11, 1918

Kinross (centre) after the investiture

PEARKES, George Randolph

V.C.	Passchendaele, October 30th-31st, 1917
Born	Watford, Hertfordshire, England, February 26th, 1888
Unit	5th Canadian Mounted Rifles Battalion, C.E.F.
	Residing at Victoria, B.C.

For most conspicuous bravery and skilful handling of the troops under his command during the capture and consolidation of considerably more than the objectives allotted to him, in an attack.

Just prior to the advance Maj. Pearkes was wounded in the left thigh. Regardless of his wound, he continued to lead his men with the utmost gallantry, despite many obstacles.

At a particular stage of the attack his further advance was threatened by a strong point which was an objective of the battalion on his left, but which they had not succeeded in capturing. Quickly appreciating the situation, he captured and held this point, thus enabling his further advance to be successfully pushed forward....

He showed throughout a supreme contempt of danger and wonderful powers of control and leading.

London Gazette, January 11, 1918

[Pearkes was hit by shrapnel and knocked down. He describes his feelings at the time:] I thought "Now I've got it!" There seemed to be a little uncertainty among the men alongside me, whether they should go on when I'd been hit. For a moment I had visions of going back wounded and I said to myself: "This can't be. I've got to go on for a while anyway, wounded or not." So I clambered to my feet and I found a stiffness in my left thigh but I was able to move forward ... then the rest of the company all came forward. [After seizing the objectives, and holding them against counter-attacks throughout the day, the survivors (who were by then reduced to a mere handful) were relieved when darkness made it possible. One of them, A. C. Philps, wrote to Pearkes' biographer:] "I would have followed him through hell if I had to."

Information supplied by Dr. R. H. Roy, biographer of General Pearkes

George Randolph Pearkes

BARRON, Colin Fraser

V.C.	Passchendaele, November 6th, 1917
Born	Baldavie, Renfrewshire, Scotland, September 20th, 1893
Unit	3rd Battalion, C.E.F.
Died	Toronto, August 15th, 1958

[At Passchendaele, on the front of the 3rd Battalion] a machine gun nest caused serious trouble. For a long time this strongpoint spat forth fire at the least sign of movement. Its guns inflicted many casualties and held up the advance for a considerable time. Covering fire was provided with good effect by riflemen who engaged targets and inflicted casualties at up to a hundred yards, but it was the action of one corporal who wormed his way forward on his belly that perhaps did most to decide the day.

Corporal Colin Fraser Barron got close enough to the enemy machine gun post to toss some bombs into it, silencing the guns. Then he charged the post, found most of the enemy dead, and killed or captured the remainder. For his actions that morning Corporal Barron was subsequently awarded the Victoria Cross.

Battle Royal

Silencing a strongpoint

ROBERTSON, James Peter

V.C.	Passchendaele, November 6th, 1917 (Posthumous)
Born	Albion Mines, Pictou, Nova Scotia, October 26th, 1883
Unit	27th Battalion, C.E.F.
Died	November 6th, 1917

[During the final assault on the village of Passchendaele a German machine gun, on the left flank of the 27th Battalion, held up the advance with fire at point blank range.]

Private Robertson crossed the open line of fire alone, and running round the flank of the position, leapt the barbed wire and got in with his bayonet among the garrison.... They fled.... But Robertson did not intend to let them escape.... Seizing the captured gun, he swung it about and opened fire on the running men, killing most of them.... Then, bearing the captured gun with him, he continued ... [into the village].

During the consolidation, Private Robertson had been busy with his new machine-gun, but, seeing two of our men lying wounded well in advance of the line, ... he went forward to bring them in. He got in successfully enough with the first man.... In spite of a veritable storm of bullets, Robertson went out again. He fell before reaching the second man — he was probably hit — but picking himself up, he continued his way, and secured his wounded comrade. Slipping on the sticky mud, nearly exhausted, he stuck to his man, and had put him down close to our line, when an unlucky shell exploded near by, killing him instantly.

Thirty Canadian V.Cs.

James Peter Robertson

Lieutenant-Governor Brett of Alberta presented the Victoria Cross to Peter Robertson's mother at Medicine Hat in April, 1918 and noted that while money can buy many things, the Victoria Cross can be won only by valour and service.

The Medicine Hat News, June 29, 1967

STRACHAN, Harcus

V.C.	Masnières, France, November 20th, 1917
Born	Borrowstounness, Scotland, November 7th, 1889
Unit	Fort Garry Horse, C.E.F.
	Residing in Vancouver

For most conspicuous bravery and leadership during operations.

He took command of the squadron of his regiment when the squadron leader . . . was killed. Lt. Strachan led the squadron through the enemy line of machine-gun posts, and then, with the surviving men, led the charge on the enemy battery, killing seven of the gunners with his sword.

London Gazette, December 18, 1917

The men went forward at the gallop to an objective dear to any cavalryman's heart. A battery of field guns lay before them. A good horse, firm ground and guns to be taken — a cavalryman wants no more. The Canadians charged down upon them, and in a moment were among the guns, riding the gunners down or sabring them as they stood. . . . There was a brief mêlée of plunging horses and stumbling artillerymen. Then the business was finished.

The Victoria Cross

All the gunners having been killed and the battery silenced, he rallied his men and fought his way back at night through the enemy's line, bringing all unwounded men safely in, together with 15 prisoners.

The operation — which resulted in the silencing of an enemy battery, the killing of the whole battery personnel and many infantry, and the cutting of three main lines of telephone communication two miles in rear of the enemy's front line — was only rendered possible by the outstanding gallantry and fearless leading of this officer.

London Gazette, December 18, 1917

Strachan leads troopers of the Fort Garry Horse near Cambrai

De WIND, Edmund

V.C.	Near Grougie, France, March 21st, 1918 (Posthumous)
Born	Comber, County Down, Ireland, December 11th, 1883
Unit	31st Battalion, C.E.F., later 15th Battalion, Royal Irish Rifles (British Army)
Died	March 21st, 1918

[A letter written by De Wind, 1 Nov., 1915:]

I am now in the Machine Gun Section of the 31st Battalion and like the work very much, and we have an awfully nice willing bunch of fellows in it. We have been in first and second line trenches for over a month, and at present are having a week's rest in an old farm house near a village. Our buildings are pretty well intact, but it is awful to see miles of trenches and sand-bag parapets all around. It will be two or three decades after the war before things are in any sort of good shape. It is beautiful, rich, mixed farming country, but a good lot of rain and fog in the fall apparently. "Sunny Alberta" will look mighty good again to those of us who are lucky enough to pull through.

Letters from the Front

For most conspicuous bravery and self-sacrifice on the 21st March, 1918, at the Race Course Redoubt, near Grougie.

For seven hours he held this most important post, and though twice wounded and practically single-handed, he maintained his position until another section could be got to his help.

On two occasions, with two N.C.O.'s only, he got out on top under heavy machine-gun and rifle fire, and cleared the enemy out of the trench, killing many.

He continued to repel attack after attack until he was mortally wounded and collapsed. His valour, self-sacrifice and example were of the highest order.

London Gazette, May 15, 1919

Edmund De Wind

McLEOD, Alan Arnett

V.C.	Albert (Somme), France, March 27th, 1918
Born	Stonewall, Manitoba, April 20th, 1899
Service	Royal Flying Corps
Died	Winnipeg, November 6th, 1918

[2nd Lieutenant Alan McLeod won the V.C. at eighteen years of age when flying a slow, two-seater, Armstrong Whitworth bomber-reconnaissance machine which had "the aerodynamics of a cow." He and his observer, Lieutenant Hammond, were attacked by a fast German fighter which they shot down. Seven more Fokker triplanes descended; Hammond shot one down.]

We jumped up to about five or six thousand feet [McLeod wrote to his parents], and foolishly stayed to scrap with them ... we fought for a while. ... Then they got us. By this time I had a few bullets in me, and they were beginning to hurt, when our machine burst into flames.

Letter dated April 8, 1918

[The entire floor of the aircraft fell out. McLeod climbed on to the wing, controlled the aircraft from there, and managed to flatten out for a crash landing while Hammond climbed out on the edge of the rear cockpit and perched there; from that position he shot down a third Fokker which had approached too close to the stricken aircraft.]

The story of two men, coming down in flames, flying and fighting with the bottom literally ripped out of their plane — the pilot perched on the wing root with his hand on the control column, the observer sitting on the edge of the cockpit and somehow managing to fire his gun — became part of the tradition of the service.

Knights of the Air

[They landed in No Man's Land, where the bombs and ammunition started to explode. McLeod, with five wounds, dragged his companion, wounded in six places, clear; but he was hit once more and collapsed from loss of blood. South African troops evacuated them from the front line after dark.]

From *Knights of the Air*
Illustration by William Wheeler

FLOWERDEW, Gordon Muriel

V.C.	Bois de Moreuil, France, March 30th, 1918 (Posthumous)
Born	Billingford, Norfolk, England, January 2nd, 1885
Unit	Lord Strathcona's Horse (Royal Canadians), C.E.F.
Died	March 31st, 1918

[Since the opening of the great German spring offensive of March, 1918, the Canadian Cavalry Brigade had been fighting rearguard actions, mounted and on foot. On March 30th, the Brigade received orders to seize a wood, known as the Bois de Moreuil.]

[Flowerdew's] squadron rounded the corner of the wood at a gallop, to cut off the retreat of the enemy on the eastern side. They were nearly at the destination when suddenly ... they saw ... two lines of Germans facing them. There were about sixty Germans in each line, and machine-guns were posted in the centre and on the flanks of both.... Immediately the enemy saw the horsemen they opened fire.

Flowerdew quickly ordered a troop under Lieut. Harvey, V.C., to dismount and carry out a special movement. With the remaining men he charged the German lines.

From the enemy machine-guns came a concentrated stream of fire on the rushing cavalry.... It was a return to the days when battles were decided by the strength of men's arms. It was the charge of the Light Brigade over again, on a smaller scale — smaller in physical weight of onslaught and opposition, but equal in spirit.

The Germans stood up boldly to the attack. They never expected that the horsemen would penetrate into their midst.... Through the first line went the squadron, across the intervening space and through the second line, cutting down the enemy as they passed. Behind the second line they wheeled and rode through again full tilt. Over seventy per cent. of the attackers were casualties, but the fury of the charge was more than the Germans could face. They broke and fled. [Flowerdew, shot through both thighs, died next day.]

Thirty Canadian V.Cs.

"Charge of Flowerdew's Squadron"
From oil by Sir Alfred Munnings. Canadian War Museum

McKEAN, George Burdon

V.C.	Gavrelle Sector (near Vimy Ridge), April 27th-28th, 1918
Born	Wellington, Durham, England, July 4th, 1888
Unit	14th Battalion, C.E.F.
Died	England, November 28th, 1926

[During a raid on the enemy's forward positions] Hussar Trench was manned by a garrison which decided to fight to the end. Choosing a block in the trench as a suitable point for defence, the Germans held back the Canadians with bombs and rifle fire. Three times Lieut. McKean's party exhausted its supply of bombs and sent back to the Royal Montreal front line for more. And still the German block barred all progress. Realizing that time was slipping by, Lieut. McKean bade his men stand clear. Revolver in hand, he then ran, and dived head first over the obstruction. Crashing into a German, who seemed to be the enemy leader, Lieut. McKean bore him to earth, and killed him with a revolver shot. [He also shot a German who was rushing at him with fixed bayonet.] Simultaneously, the men of 'E' Group swarmed over the barricade, swept aside opposition, and advanced.

The Royal Montreal Regiment

George Burdon McKean
Painting by F. H. Varley. Canadian War Museum

BOURKE, Rowland Richard Louis

V.C.	Ostend, Belgium, May 10th, 1918
Born	London, England, November 28th, 1885
Service	Royal Naval Volunteer Reserve
Died	Esquimalt, B.C., August 29th, 1958

[Bourke tried to enlist in the Canadian services when war broke out, but was rejected because of defective eyesight. After joining the Royal Naval Volunteer Reserve in England he commanded a motor launch during a naval attempt to block the port of Ostend, then used by the Germans, in May, 1918. After the raid Bourke searched the smoke-filled harbour for British survivors and, despite machine-gun bursts at close range and heavy shellfire, rescued one officer and two seamen. His launch was hit in fifty-five places, two of the crew killed and others wounded. Bourke, however, brought her out at reduced speed. He turned the survivors over to a monitor which took his launch in tow.]

Based on the *London Gazette*, August 28, 1918

"The Blocking of Ostend," by G. H. Davis

KAEBLE,* Joseph

V.C.	Neuville-Vitasse, France, June 8th-9th, 1918 (Posthumous)
Born	St. Moise, Quebec, May 5th, 1893
Unit	22nd Battalion, C.E.F.
Died	June 9th, 1918

During an intense bombardment Cpl. Kaeble remained at the parapet with his Lewis gun shouldered ready for action, the field of fire being very short. As soon as the barrage lifted from the front line, about fifty of the enemy advanced towards his post. By this time the whole of his section except one had become casualties. Cpl. Kaeble jumped over the parapet, and holding his Lewis gun at the hip, emptied one magazine after another into the advancing enemy and, although wounded several times by fragments of shells and bombs, he continued to fire, and entirely blocked the enemy by his determined stand. Finally, firing all the time, he fell backwards into the trench, mortally wounded. While lying on his back in the trench he fired his last cartridges over the parapet after the retreating Germans, and before losing consciousness shouted, "Tenez bon, mes vieux, ne les laissez pas passer, il faut les arrêter!"

London Gazette, September 16, 1918

Joseph Kaeble
Pencil drawing by Alfred Bastien. Canadian War Museum

* His family name was Keable but the spelling "Kaeble" is used in the records and this has become the "official" spelling.

CROAK,* John Bernard

V.C.	Amiens, France, August 8th, 1918 (Posthumous)
Born	Little Bay, Newfoundland, May 18th, 1892
Unit	13th Battalion, C.E.F.
Died	August 8th, 1918

It was ... in attack that Private Croak distinguished himself. He bombed and silenced a machine-gun nest which he had encountered when he had become separated from his section and he took the gun and the crew prisoners. Soon afterwards he was severely wounded, but ... he refused to desist. When the private had rejoined his platoon a very strong point, containing several machine guns, was encountered. Croak, because of his wound, had every excuse for remaining behind, but his splendid courage impelled him to dash forward alone. His example was like a flash of fire to a powder-train, and the rest of his platoon instantly followed him "in a brilliant charge." Croak was the first to reach the trench-line, and into this he led his restless men, capturing three machine guns and bayoneting or taking the entire garrison. This fine soldier was again wounded, so severely that he died.

Times History of the War, vol. xvii.

John Bernard Croak

* The Newfoundland spelling of this name is "Croke" and that is how it appears on John Bernard's birth certificate. He enlisted, however, as "Croak," and in view of the many records containing this spelling we have retained it.

GOOD, Herman James

V.C.	Near Amiens, August 8th, 1918
Born	South Bathurst, New Brunswick, November 29th, 1887
Unit	13th Battalion, C.E.F.
Died	Bathurst, N.B., April 18th, 1969

Corporal H. J. Good, ... alone, charged a nest of three machine guns and killed or captured the crews. Later, when the advance had penetrated deep into the German lines and was pushing forward to its final objective, this same N.C.O. discovered a battery of 5.9 inch guns, in action and pounding the Canadian advance and rear. To charge a battery of 5.9's with a force which consisted of himself and three privates might seem the act of a madman, but Corp. Good realized that the gun crews were not trained in hand-to-hand fighting and that, once at grips, he and his stout-hearted companions would have an advantage sufficient, possibly, to offset their appalling inferiority in numbers. Accordingly he and his party charged. What the German gunners thought when this assault was launched, no man will ever know. Perhaps in the drill and text books they had studied no instructions were given as to procedure when four Canadian Highlanders charged a battery with the obvious intent of doing bodily harm. Be that as it may, the battery surrendered and the four Highlanders found themselves owners of three excellent guns and masters of a good sized batch of prisoners.

The 13th Battalion Royal Highlanders of Canada

Corporal Good (Left)

MINER, Harry Garnet Bedford

V.C.	Demuin, France, August 8th, 1918 (Posthumous)
Born	Cedar Springs, Ontario, June 24th, 1891
Unit	58th Battalion, C.E.F.
Died	August 8th, 1918

During 'B' Company's initial attack on the German outpost lines, Corporal H. G. B. Miner, although severely wounded in the head and shoulder, refused to withdraw but led his section into the middle of the German position. When an enemy machine gun post held up the advance, Corporal Miner rushed it single-handed, killed the entire crew, and turned the captured gun on the enemy. Subsequently, he and two others put a second machine gun out of action. Corporal Miner then rushed a German bombing post, bayoneted two of its garrison, and put the remainder to flight. At this post he was mortally wounded by German stick grenades, and later in the day he died of his wounds.

Battle Royal

Turning a captured machine gun on the enemy

BRILLANT, Jean

V.C.	Méharicourt (near Amiens), August 8th-9th, 1918 (Posthumous)
Born	Assametquaghan, Quebec, March 15th, 1890
Unit	22nd Battalion, C.E.F.
Died	August 10th, 1918

On the first day of operations shortly after the attack had begun, his company left flank was held up by an enemy machine-gun. Lt. Brillant rushed and captured the machine-gun, personally killing two of the enemy crew. Whilst doing this, he was wounded, but refused to leave his command.

Later on the same day, his company was held up by heavy machine-gun fire. He reconnoitred the ground personally, organised a party of two platoons and rushed straight for the machine-gun nest. Here 150 enemy and fifteen machine-guns were captured, Lt. Brillant personally killing five of the enemy, and being wounded a second time. He had this wound dressed immediately, and again refused to leave his company.

Subsequently this gallant officer detected a field gun firing on his men over open sights. He immediately organised and led a "rushing" party towards the gun. After progressing about 600 yards, he was again seriously wounded. In spite of this third wound, he continued to advance for some 200 yards more.

London Gazette, September 27, 1918

"Je suis fini," ... dit le blessé, "prends charge de la compagnie, car je sais que ça ne sera pas long."

Histoire du 22e Bataillon canadien-français

[He then fell unconscious from exhaustion and loss of blood, dying on the following day.]

Colonel Jules Brillant places a wreath at the monument erected in memory of his brother in Jean Brillant Park, Montreal, during the summer of 1971

ZENGEL, Raphael Louis

V.C.	Amiens, August 9th, 1918
Born	Faribault, Minnesota, U.S.A., November 11th, 1894
Unit	5th Battalion, C.E.F.
	Residing at Errington, B.C.

He was leading his platoon gallantly forward to the attack, but had not gone far when he realised that a gap had occurred on his flank, and that an enemy machine gun was firing at close range into the advancing line. Grasping the situation, he rushed forward some 200 yards ahead of the platoon, tackled the machine-gun emplacement, killed the officer and operator of the gun, and dispersed the crew. By his boldness and prompt action he undoubtedly saved the lives of many of his comrades.

Later, when the battalion was held up by very heavy machine-gun fire, he displayed much tactical skill and directed his fire with destructive results. Shortly afterwards he was rendered unconscious for a few minutes by an enemy shell, but on recovering consciousness he at once continued to direct harassing fire on the enemy.

Sjt. Zengel's work throughout the attack was excellent, and his utter disregard for personal safety, and the confidence he inspired in all ranks, greatly assisted in bringing the attack to a successful end.

London Gazette, September 27, 1918

Raphael Louis Zengel

BRERETON, Alexander Picton

V.C.	Amiens, August 9th, 1918
Born	Oak River, Manitoba, November 13th, 1892
Unit	8th Battalion, C.E.F.
	Residing at Fort St. John, B.C.

A line of hostile machine guns opened fire suddenly on his platoon, which was in an exposed position, and no cover available. This gallant N.C.O. at once appreciated the critical situation and realised that unless something was done at once the platoon would be annihilated. On his own initiative, without a moment's delay, and alone, he sprang forward and reached one of the hostile machine-gun posts, where he shot the man operating the machine gun and bayonetted the next one who attempted to operate it, whereupon nine others surrendered to him.

Cpl. Brereton's action was a splendid example of resource and bravery, and not only undoubtedly saved many of his comrades' lives, but also inspired his platoon to charge and capture the five remaining posts.

London Gazette, September 27, 1918

"Bayonet Attack"

COPPINS, Frederick George

V.C.	Hackett Wood (Hatchet Wood), Amiens, August 9th, 1918
Born	London, England, October 25th, 1889
Unit	8th Battalion, C.E.F.
Died	Livermore, California, U.S.A., March 30th, 1963

The presentation of Coppins' V.C. to the Valour Road Branch of the Royal Canadian Legion, Winnipeg, during 1965

The details of the awards to Corporal Coppins and Corporal Brereton so closely resembled each other that there could be no doubt that these two members of the Manitoba Regiment were concerned in the same heroic undertaking. They found themselves in desperate case; but so far from shirking danger they courted it, with the happy result that they were the means of saving many lives and of materially helping military objectives. During an attack Corporal Coppins's platoon unexpectedly came under the fire of numerous machine guns. The platoon could neither advance nor retire, nor was any cover available, and it was clear that unless the hostile guns were silenced instantly the platoon would be annihilated. The corporal unhesitatingly, and acting on his own initiative, called on four men to follow him. They readily obeyed, and all rushed straight for the machine guns, from which an intense fire came. The four men were killed and the corporal was wounded, but despite his wounds he reached the guns alone and killed the operator of the first gun and three of the crew, and made prisoners of four others, who surrendered. In spite of his wound Corporal Coppins continued with his platoon to the final objective, and did not leave the line until it had been made secure and he had been ordered to do so. This, like Corporal Brereton's, was an uncommonly fine exploit, one of many of which some idea had been given in the accounts of Canadian dash and endurance in the main theatre of the war.

Times History of the War, vol. xvii

TAIT, James Edward

V.C.	Amiens, August 8th-11th, 1918 (Posthumous)
Born	Dumfries, Scotland, May 27th, 1886
Unit	78th Battalion, C.E.F.
Died	August 11th, 1918

The advance having been checked by intense machine-gun fire, Lt. Tait rallied his company and led it forward with consummate skill and dash under a hail of bullets. A concealed machine-gun, however, continued to cause many casualties. Taking a rifle and bayonet, Lt. Tait dashed forward alone and killed the enemy gunner. Inspired by his example his men rushed the position, capturing twelve machine-guns and twenty prisoners. His valorous action cleared the way for his battalion to advance.

Later when the enemy counter-attacked our positions under intense artillery bombardment, this gallant officer displayed outstanding courage and leadership, and though mortally wounded by a shell, continued to direct and aid his men until his death.

London Gazette, September 27, 1918

Machine-gun menace removed

DINESEN, Thomas

V.C.	Parvillers (near Amiens), August 12th, 1918
Born	Rungsted, Denmark, August 9th, 1892
Unit	42nd Battalion, C.E.F.
	Residing in Denmark

Throughout the action he was the spearhead of 'D' Company's thrust far into the enemy's lines. His work with the bayonet was deadly and his carefree courage was the keynote of the spirit of the men. . . . Time after time he led the way into the midst of groups of enemy, wielding bayonet and clubbed rifle with irresistible effect. Repeatedly, also, he rushed forward alone in the face of machine-gun fire from which it seemed impossible to escape unhurt and personally put the guns out of action.

It was from the testimony of the men themselves that it was afterwards learned that Private Thomas Dinesen of 'D' Company was the outstanding figure of these memorable days.

The 42nd Battalion

Five times in succession he rushed forward alone, and single-handed put hostile machine guns out of action, accounting for twelve of the enemy with bomb and bayonet.

London Gazette, October 26, 1918

Thomas Dinesen

SPALL, Robert

V.C.	Parvillers, August 12th-13th, 1918 (Posthumous)
Born	Ealing, Essex, England, March 5th, 1890
Unit	Princess Patricia's Canadian Light Infantry, C.E.F.
Died	August 13th, 1918

[Sergeant Robert Spall] took a Lewis gun and standing on the parapet fired upon the advancing enemy, inflicting most severe casualties. He then came down the trench directing the men into a sap seventy-five yards from the enemy. Picking up another Lewis gun he again climbed the parapet and with his fire held up the enemy.

Princess Patricia's Canadian Light Infantry

It was while holding up the enemy at this point that he was killed.

Sjt. Spall deliberately gave his life in order to extricate his platoon from a most difficult situation, and it was owing to his bravery that the platoon was saved.

London Gazette, October 26, 1918

Robert Spall

RUTHERFORD, Charles Smith

V.C.	Monchy-le-Preux, France, August 26th, 1918
Born	Colborne, Ontario, January 9th, 1892
Unit	5th Canadian Mounted Rifles Battalion, C.E.F.
	Residing at Keswick, Ontario

Lieutenant Rutherford, when doing desperate work against "pill-boxes," made hauls of 80 prisoners and some machine guns, spread dismay and confusion amongst the enemy, and did much to press home an attack on a very strong position. . . . He was commanding an assaulting party when he found himself a considerable distance ahead of his men. At the same moment he saw a strong and fully-armed party of the enemy outside a pill-box ahead of him. . . . The lieutenant beckoned to . . . the Germans with his revolver to come to him, and the Germans, not to be outdone, for once, in courtesy, "waved to him to come to them." The embarrassing situation was relieved by the officer boldly going to the Germans; but it became intensified when he told them that they were prisoners. . . . The enemy officer disputed the fact and asked Rutherford to enter the pill-box. A Canadian was not likely to be caught in such an obvious trap and Rutherford . . . declined the invitation. "By masterly bluff," however, he managed to persuade the Germans that they were surrounded, and the whole party of 45, including two officers, with three machine guns, surrendered to him. Having bagged the German officer, Lieutenant Rutherford further employed his wiles to the extent of inducing the captive to stop the fire of a hostile machine gun close by, after which the victor was smart enough to hasten the advance of his men to his support. Subsequently attacking another pill-box with a Lewis gun section, the lieutenant took 35 more prisoners, with machine guns.

Times History of the War, vol. xviii

Charles Smith Rutherford

CLARK-KENNEDY, William Hew

V.C.	Wancourt, France, August 27th-28th, 1918
Born	Dunskay, Ayrshire, Scotland, March 3rd, 1880
Unit	24th Battalion, C.E.F.
Died	October 25th, 1961

[At 12:30 p.m., the barrage on the 2nd Canadian Divisional front opened and at once the Canadian troops, leaving the trenches in which they had passed the night, resumed the attack of the previous day. At midday] the attack of the 24th Battalion ... encountered bitter artillery and machine-gun resistance, the casualties in the early stages of the advance including the Commanding Officer [Lt.-Col. Clark-Kennedy], who fell with a shattered leg. ...

Knowledge of the situation was brought to Brigade Headquarters by Sergt. J. N. Swift ... who reported that the unit was definitely held up some 200 yards short of the first objective. Sergt. Swift added that the casualties had been severe but that the Commanding Officer, though badly injured and quite unable to move, was in touch with the situation and was carrying out his duties to the full extent that circumstances would permit. ...

At 5:30 p.m. Lieut.-Col. Clark-Kennedy realized that the situation had stabilized on his front and consented to be carried back from the shell-hole, whence, for hours, he had exercised command.

The 24th Battalion

William Hew Clark-Kennedy

NUNNEY, Claude Joseph Patrick

V.C.	Drocourt-Quéant Line, France, September 1st-2nd, 1918 (Posthumous)
Born	Hastings, England, December 24th, 1892
Unit	38th Battalion, C.E.F.
Died	September 18th, 1918

The record concerning Private Nunney was notable because it did not specify any particular act of valour, but was a plain statement of an exhibition of cool, consistent fearlessness which was priceless as an example. The private won his fame during the operation against the Drocourt-Quéant line on September 1 and 2. On the 1st, when his battalion was in the vicinity of Vis-en-Artois, preparatory to the advance, the Germans laid down a heavy barrage and counter-attacked. Nunney was at this time at company headquarters and he at once, on his own initiative, proceeded through the barrage to the company outpost lines, "going from post to post and encouraging the men by his own fearless example." The Germans were repulsed and a critical situation was saved. The private's dash during the attack on the 2nd continually placed him in advance of his companions, and his conduct undoubtedly helped greatly to carry the company forward to its objectives. Nunney carried on in this determined fashion until he was severely wounded.

Times History of the War, vol. xix

Claude Joseph Patrick Nunney

KNIGHT, Arthur George

V.C.	Villers-lez-Cagnicourt (near Arras, France), September 2nd, 1918 (Posthumous)
Born	Hayward's Heath, Sussex, England, June 26th, 1886
Unit	10th Battalion, C.E.F.
Died	September 3rd, 1918

Sergeant Knight, before he was fatally wounded, showed extraordinary courage as an individual fighter. A bombing section which he was leading being held up, he dashed forward alone, and after bayoneting several machine gunners and trench mortar crews he forced the rest to retire in confusion; then, bringing forward a Lewis gun, he inflicted many casualties on the retreating enemy. His platoon went in pursuit and the sergeant, seeing about 30 of the enemy go into a deep tunnel leading off the trench, again dashed forward alone and killed an officer and two non-commissioned officers and made 20 prisoners; after which, once more single-handed, he routed another hostile party.

Times History of the War, vol. xviii

Arthur George Knight

METCALF, William Henry

V.C.	Arras, September 2nd, 1918
Born	Waite Township, Maine, U.S.A., January 29th, 1885
Unit	16th Battalion, C.E.F.
Died	Lewiston, Maine, August 8th, 1968

There we were. Every time we exposed ourselves they opened fire on us. . . . We decided before making another move to wait for a tank. . . . We signalled to it with our helmets, but the tank did not see us. . . . Suddenly a heavy fire started from the trench in front of us. We looked up and there we saw the tank with Lance-Corporal Metcalf walking beside it, pointing with his signal flags in our direction. . . .

When the tank came to within three hundred feet of the German wire [writes . . . another witness of Metcalf's exploit], a heavy machine-gun fire was opened upon it from the front trench. Corporal Metcalf jumped up from the shell-hole where he was and with his flags pointing towards the enemy's trench, led the tank towards it and then along it. The enemy kept heavy machine-gun fire on the tank and as it got close to the trench commenced to throw at it clusters of bombs tied together. When we afterwards got into the trench, we found seventeen German machine-guns at the same place, and all of them had been well used. How Metcalf escaped being shot to pieces has always been a wonder to me.

The History of the 16th Battalion

[However, he was wounded.] Later . . . he continued to advance until ordered to get into a shell hole and have his wounds dressed.

London Gazette, November 15, 1918

"Tank destroying a German machine-gun post"

PECK, Cyrus Wesley

V.C.	Villers-lez-Cagnicourt, September 2nd, 1918
Born	Hopewell Hill, New Brunswick, April 26th, 1871
Unit	16th Battalion, C.E.F.
Died	Sidney, Vancouver Island, B.C., September 27th, 1956

For most conspicuous bravery and skilful leading when in attack under intense fire.

His command quickly captured the first objective, but progress to the further objective was held up by enemy machine-gun fire on his right flank.

The situation being critical in the extreme, Colonel Peck pushed forward and made a personal reconnaissance under heavy machine-gun and sniping fire. . . .

Having reconnoitred the position he returned, reorganised his battalion, and, acting on the knowledge personally gained, pushed them forward and arranged to protect his flanks. He then went out under the most intense artillery and machine-gun fire, intercepted the Tanks, gave them the necessary directions, pointing out where they were to make for, and thus paved the way for a Canadian Infantry battalion to push forward. To this battalion he subsequently gave requisite support.

London Gazette, November 15, 1918

[An eyewitness:] We were firing smoke bombs in an endeavour to conceal our positions as much as possible, when a tank, which had been following us up stopped, possibly thirty yards in our rear, and proceeded to turn around to go back.

An attempt was made to stop the tank but with no success. Colonel Peck, observing what had happened, left the shell hole where he was taking cover and under heavy machine gun fire ran back to the tank. He stood directly in front of it. He forced it to turn around. . . .

I do not know how the Colonel escaped being riddled by bullets.

The History of the 16th Battalion

After the Investiture at Buckingham Palace

HUTCHESON, Bellenden Seymour

V.C.	Drocourt-Quéant Support Line, France, September 2nd, 1918
Born	Mount Carmel, Illinois, U.S.A., December 16th, 1883
Service	Canadian Army Medical Corps (attached 75th Battalion, C.E.F.)
Died	Cairo, Illinois, April 9th, 1954

Captain Hutcheson, as a doctor, performed many brave acts by which many lives were saved, though only two or three of these were recorded in the official story. His particular displays of self sacrificing courage were on September 2, when, with the battalion, he went through the Drocourt-Quéant Support Line under the most intense fire from artillery, rifles and machine guns. The officer showed that utter disregard of his own safety which had become almost a characteristic of our Army surgeons, and he unhesitatingly and coolly remained on the field until every wounded man had received attention. "Under terrific machine-gun and shell fire" Captain Hutcheson dressed the wounds of a seriously wounded officer and, with the help of his own men and prisoners he evacuated him to safety, in spite of the fact that the bearer party suffered heavy casualties. Immediately after this exhibition of fortitude and humanity the captain, in full view of the Germans, and still under heavy fire from rifles and machine guns, rushed forward to tend a wounded sergeant, and having placed him in a shell hole, he dressed his wounds. "Captain Hutcheson performed many similar gallant acts."

Times History of the War, vol. xix

"Tending the wounded"

YOUNG, John Francis

V.C.	Dury-Arras Sector, September 2nd, 1918
Born	Kidderminster, England, January 14th, 1893
Unit	87th Battalion, C.E.F.
Died	Ste. Agathe, Quebec, November 7th, 1929

Acting as stretcher-bearer attached to 'D' Company of the 87th Bn., Quebec Regiment ... [his] company in the advance over the ridge suffered heavy casualties from shell and machine-gun fire.

Pte. Young, in spite of the complete absence of cover, without the least hesitation went out, and in the open fire-swept ground dressed the wounded. Having exhausted his stock of dressings, on more than one occasion he returned, under intense fire, to his company headquarters for a further supply. This work he continued for over an hour, displaying throughout the most absolute fearlessness.

To his courageous conduct must be ascribed the saving of the lives of many of his comrades.

Later, when the fire had somewhat slackened, he organised and led stretcher parties to bring in the wounded whom he had dressed.

All through the operations of 2nd, 3rd, and 4th September Pte. Young continued to show the greatest valour and devotion to duty.

London Gazette, December 14, 1918

J. M. Miller, *The People's War Book*

RAYFIELD, Walter Leigh

V.C.   Arras, September 2nd-4th, 1918
Born   Richmond-on-Thames, England, October 7th, 1881
Unit   7th Battalion, C.E.F.
Died   Toronto, February 19th, 1949

For most conspicuous bravery, devotion to duty, and initiative during the operations east of Arras from 2nd to 4th September, 1918.

Ahead of his company, he rushed a trench occupied by a large party of the enemy, personally bayoneting two and taking ten prisoners.

Later, he located and engaged with great skill, under constant rifle fire, an enemy sniper who was causing many casualties. He then rushed the section of trench from which the sniper had been operating, and so demoralised the enemy by his coolness and daring that thirty others surrendered to him.

Again, regardless of his personal safety, he left cover under heavy machine-gun fire and carried in a badly wounded comrade. His indomitable courage, cool foresight, and daring reconnaissance were invaluable to his Company Commander and an inspiration to all ranks.

London Gazette, December 14, 1918

[He set] a superb example to all ranks for coolness, courage and resource.

Short History of the 7th Battalion

Walter Leigh Rayfield

KERR, George Fraser

V.C.	Bourlon Wood (near Cambrai, France), September 27th, 1918
Born	Deseronto, Ontario, June 8th, 1894
Unit	3rd Battalion, C.E.F.
Died	Toronto, December 8th, 1929

Kerr was in command of the left support company in attack and handled it with great skill, giving timely support by outflanking a machine gun which was impeding the advance. Afterwards, near the Arras–Cambrai Road, the advance was again held up by a strong point, and this critical emergency gave Lieutenant Kerr the chance to establish his reputation as a fighter of the utmost merit. "Far in advance of his company" he rushed the strong point single-handed and with such overwhelming impetuosity that he captured four machine guns and no fewer than 31 prisoners.

Times History of the War, vol. xix

George Fraser Kerr
Seated front row, third from left

LYALL, Graham Thomson

V.C.	Bourlon Wood, September 27th, 1918
Born	Manchester, England, March 8th, 1892
Unit	102nd Battalion, C.E.F.
Died	Mersa Matruh, Egypt (serving in British Army), November 28th, 1941

On September 27th, 1918, whilst leading his platoon against Bourlon Wood, he rendered invaluable support to the leading company, which was held up by a strong point, which he captured by a flank movement, together with thirteen prisoners, one field gun and four machine guns.

Later, his platoon, now much weakened by casualties, was held up by machine guns at the southern end of Bourlon Wood. Collecting any man available, he led them towards the strong point, and, springing forward alone, rushed the position single-handed and killed the officer in charge, subsequently capturing at this point forty-five prisoners and five machine guns. Having made good his final objective, with a further capture of forty-seven prisoners, he consolidated his position and thus protected the remainder of the company.

On October 1st, in the neighbourhood of Blécourt, when in command of a weak company, by skilful dispositions he captured a strongly defended position, which yielded eighty prisoners and seventeen machine guns.

During two days of operations Lt. Lyall captured in all 3 officers, 182 other ranks, 26 machine guns, and one field gun, exclusive of heavy casualties inflicted. He showed throughout the utmost valour and high powers of command.

London Gazette, December 14, 1918

Lyall, with his English relatives, after the investiture

HONEY, Samuel Lewis

V.C.	Bourlon Wood, September 27th-30th, 1918 (Posthumous)
Born	Conn, Ontario, February 9th, 1894
Unit	78th Battalion, C.E.F.
Died	September 30th, 1918

Bourlon Wood was the scene of the operations in which, from September 27 . . ., Lieutenant Honey played an important part. On the 27th, when all his company officers had become casualties, Honey took command, and under very severe fire skilfully carried out reorganisation. Continuing the advance with great dash he gained the objective. He now found that his company was suffering casualties from enfilade machine-gun fire, whereupon he followed the example which had been so often set — he located and rushed, single-handed, the machine-gun nest, and captured the guns and 10 prisoners. Lieutenant Honey afterwards repelled four counter-attacks, and after dark, again went out alone, and having located an enemy post he led a party which captured it and three guns. There was no falling off in the high character of the work which Honey set himself to do. With great skill and daring he led his company on September 29 against a strong German position, and . . . continued his display of heroism and devotion. This gallant officer died of wounds received during the last day of the attack by his battalion.

Times History of the War, vol. xix

Samuel Lewis Honey

GREGG, Milton Fowler

V.C.	Near Cambrai, September 27th-October 1st, 1918
Born	Mountain Dale, New Brunswick, April 10th, 1892
Unit	The Royal Canadian Regiment
	Residing at Sussex, N.B.

Faced with the great belts of enemy wire and under the pounding of the German barrage, Lieut. Gregg ... crawled forward alone to find how an entry into the Marcoing Line could be effected.... After a prolonged and dangerous search, Lieut. Gregg found a narrow gap in the wire through which one man at a time might pass....

Reaching the gap in the wire, he advanced ... and finally dropped into the Marcoing Line, where ... he was soon joined by a small group of his company.

Lieut. Gregg led ... a deadly attack with bombs on the first German strong point to the right. Though outnumbered, the Canadian party overcame the enemy machine-gun crews and ... forced the occupants of a deep dugout to surrender.... It yielded no less than three officers and 45 men....

With the help of ... reinforcements point after point was taken, until approximately one-half of the Marcoing Line on ... [Gregg's] front had been wrested from the enemy, an amazing feat of arms to be performed by ... a mere handful of men.

[The Germans counter-attacked.] The party used up its own bombs, used all the enemy bombs it could find, and finally crushed the German attack with a supply provided in the nick of time by Lieut. Gregg. This officer, though painfully wounded, had realized that a shortage of bombs would involve the annihilation of his party, and to obtain a supply had crawled back through the gap in the wire to where the main body ... was stationed.

The Royal Canadian Regiment

A gap in the wire

MacGREGOR, John

V.C.	Near Cambrai, September 29th-October 3rd, 1918
Born	Cawdor, Nairnshire, Scotland, February 11th, 1888
Unit	2nd Canadian Mounted Rifles Battalion, C.E.F.
Died	Powell River, B.C., June 9th, 1952

Captain MacGregor was another instance of a wounded fighter carrying on in spite of all difficulties and dangers, and of a man who, though *hors de combat*, yet succeeded in maintaining the high standard of leadership and devotion which he had set himself. His courage and endurance were shown near Cambrai, from September 29 to October 3. The whole of MacGregor's heroic work was done under heavy fire, with the added peril of acting in ... daylight. Although wounded he pushed on and located some machine guns which were checking the advance. It was broad daylight and fire came from all directions, but with rifle and bayonet, and single-handed, the captain put the German crews out of action, killing four and taking eight prisoners, the result of his energetic and successful action being that many casualties were saved and the advance was enabled to continue. Captain MacGregor reorganised his command and then performed the most valuable service of usefully supporting neighbouring troops. The Germans pulled themselves together enough to resist stubbornly, whereupon MacGregor went along the line, organised the platoons, took command of the leading waves and continued the advance. Daylight dangers seem to have had some special charm for this officer, for later, after a personal "daylight reconnaissance under heavy fire," he established his company in Neuville St. Remy, the direct result of this intrepidity being that the advance into Tilloy was greatly helped.

Times History of the War, vol. xix

John MacGregor

MERRIFIELD, William

V.C.	Abancourt, France, October 1st, 1918
Born	Brentwood, England, October 9th, 1890
Unit	4th Battalion, C.E.F.
Died	Toronto, August 8th, 1943

Sergeant Merrifield had served with "exceptional distinction" on many former occasions, and throughout the attack near Abancourt on October 1 he showed the highest qualities of valour and leadership. His acts were marked by somewhat unusual circumstances, for having single-handed attacked two machine-gun emplacements from which intense fire was holding up his men, he dashed from shell-hole to shell-hole, an undertaking which demanded rare agility and pluck. He succeeded in killing the occupants of the first post, and, although wounded, he continued to attack the second post, the occupants of which he killed with a bomb. Sergeant Merrifield's indomitable spirit made him refuse to be evacuated, and he led his platoon until he was "again severely wounded."

Times History of the War, vol. xix

William Merrifield

MITCHELL, Coulson Norman

V.C.	Canal de l'Escaut (near Cambrai), October 8th-9th, 1918
Born	Winnipeg, December 11th, 1889
Unit	4th Battalion, Canadian Engineers (1st Tunnelling Company), C.E.F.

Residing at Beaurepaire, Quebec

[Captain C. N. Mitchell, an explosives specialist in the 4th Battalion, Canadian Engineers,] had been assigned the specific job of preventing the demolition of the main Pont d'Aire bridge.... The time was 2:30 a.m.... Mitchell and his sergeant slid down the bank under the bridge having posted a sentry, Sapper Brewer, on the east side.

The beam of a flashlight revealed a large boxed charge.... The electric circuit was quickly cut and work began on the leads and charges. Suddenly there was shouting and rifle fire broke out. The enemy bridge guard, at last aware of what was happening, thought to deal with the intruders and to finish the work of destruction. Brewer had already accounted for two Germans ... Mitchell killed a third. Three dead gave the attackers pause and there was a breathing spell. After long minutes the enemy rushed in. The new attack met with heavy fire and cold steel and the Germans withdrew, leaving still more dead on the road.

Mitchell ... then ... removed six charges totalling about 500 pounds from the girders. The final episode came with the first grey of dawn, which revealed the survivors of the German demolition party ready to surrender.

History of the Corps of Royal Canadian Engineers

[Captain Mitchell and his party saved the bridge, which he well knew might at any moment have been blown by the enemy, and contributed very materially to the speed and success of the Cambrai operation.]

Coulson Norman Mitchell
Painting by Alexander Stuart-Hill. Canadian War Museum

ALGIE, Wallace Lloyd

V.C.	North-east of Cambrai, October 11th, 1918 (Posthumous)
Born	Alton, Ontario, June 10th, 1891
Unit	20th Battalion, C.E.F.
Died	October 11th, 1918

[Machine-gun] fire from Iwuy was causing many casualties in the ranks of the 20th Battalion [and] the Germans were observed bringing additional machine-guns ... towards positions from which the whole 4th Brigade front could be enfiladed, a situation which Lieutenant W. L. Algie ... determined to prevent.... His plan was to move to the left, well outside the Battalion's boundary and deny the east end of the village to the enemy.... If successful he would threaten the enemy's occupation of Iwuy and force its evacuation....

In its first rush the little party captured two machine-guns ... and destroyed their crews; following that the men set up the two captured guns and with those and their Lewis gun opened fire on advancing German squads.... After a brief struggle the survivors of the Germans were taken prisoner, an officer and ten men.

Lieutenant Algie immediately disposed his men in positions which denied the enemy the use of the eastern part of the village.... He then returned to the Battalion and collected reinforcements, but was killed while guiding them across the railway.

History of the Twentieth Canadian Battalion

Cambrai

RICKETTS, Thomas

V.C.	Ledeghem, Belgium, October 14th, 1918
Born	Middle Arm, White Bay, Newfoundland, April 15th, 1901
Unit	1st Battalion, The Royal Newfoundland Regiment
Died	St. John's, February 10th, 1967

In the platoon's Lewis gun detachment was a young soldier ... Private Thomas Ricketts, who was only seventeen years old. Two years previously he had advanced his age to eighteen in order to join the Regiment. . . .

King George introduced the youthful Ricketts to Princess Mary and others [at the investiture] saying: "This is the youngest V.C. in my army."

The Fighting Newfoundlander

The attack was temporarily held up by heavy hostile fire and the platoon to which he belonged suffered severe casualties from the fire of a battery at point-blank range.

Pte. Ricketts at once volunteered to go forward with his section commander and a Lewis gun to attempt to outflank the battery. Advancing by short rushes under heavy fire from enemy machine guns with the hostile battery, their ammunition was exhausted when still 300 yards from the battery. The enemy, seeing an opportunity to get their field guns away, began to bring up their gun teams. Pte. Ricketts, at once realising the situation, doubled back 100 yards under the heaviest machine-gun fire, procured further ammunition, and dashed back again to the Lewis gun, and by very accurate fire drove the enemy and the gun teams into a farm.

His platoon then advanced without casualties, and captured the four field guns, four machine guns and eight prisoners.

A fifth field gun was subsequently intercepted by fire and captured.

London Gazette, January 6, 1919

Thomas Ricketts

BARKER, William George

V.C.	Forêt de Mormal, France, October 27th, 1918
Born	Dauphin, Manitoba, November 3rd, 1894
Service	Royal Air Force
Died	Killed in flying accident near Ottawa, March 1st, 1930

"The spectacle of this attack was the most magnificent encounter of any sort which I ever witnessed. The ancient performances of the gladiators in the Roman arenas were far outclassed in the epic character of the successive engagements in which enemy machines, one after the other, were taken on and eliminated.... The hoarse shout, or rather the prolonged roar, which greeted the triumph of the British fighter, and which echoed across the battlefront, was never matched in Rome, nor do I think anywhere else."

The writer was General Andrew McNaughton, then... Brigadier-General commanding the Canadian Corps Heavy Artillery. From his advanced headquarters in the Valenciennes area he had witnessed one of the most spectacular air battles of all time. The pilot of the British fighter turned out to be a Canadian....

Major Barker had first attacked a German two-seater high above its own lines, causing it to break up in the air. He afterwards came under a series of attacks, at different levels, by Fokker D VII fighters. Three times he was wounded — first in one leg and then the other, and subsequently in one arm. Twice he fainted and spun down out of control, recovering only to find himself surrounded by Fokkers. Nevertheless he sent three of his opponents down in flames. He finally crash-landed his machine, a Sopwith "Snipe," in the British lines....

The fuselage is on display at the Canadian War Museum. The War Museum also holds a portrait of Barker ... and a black and white watercolour painting (opposite) by R. W. Bradford depicting Barker's great air battle.

Major Barker ... was now awarded the Victoria Cross, the citation for which concludes: "This combat, in which Major Barker destroyed four enemy machines ... brought his total successes up to fifty enemy machines destroyed."

"Major Barker and his Sopwith Snipe"

Barker's epic fight, an impression by R. W. Bradford

CAIRNS, Hugh

V.C.	Valenciennes, November 1st, 1918 (Posthumous)
Born	Ashington, Northumberland, England, December 4th, 1896
Unit	46th Battalion, C.E.F.
Died	November 2nd, 1918

[Cairns] died of wounds received in the fighting on the outskirts of Valenciennes eleven days before the Armistice. No account could more adequately describe his valour than the words of his Corps Commander, General Sir Arthur Currie, who said, in part:

"I cannot refrain from telling you of the superhuman deed of Sergeant Hugh Cairns, late of the 46th Battalion, Saskatchewan Regiment....

"A machine gun opened up on his platoon. Without a moment's hesitation, he seized a Lewis gun, and single-handed in the face of direct fire, killed the crew of five and captured the gun. Later, when the line was held up again, Sergeant Cairns rushed forward alone and killed twelve of the enemy, captured eighteen prisoners and took two machine guns.

"Then, after consolidation, he ascertained that a battle patrol was pushing out to exploit Marly. Sergeant Cairns with his Lewis gun broke open the door of a yard and came upon 60 Germans. They threw their hands up, but as the officer filed past he shot Cairns through the body. Cairns sank to his knees but continued firing. A moment later the butt of his gun was smashed and he collapsed from the loss of blood.

"The City of Valenciennes . . . decided to name a street after him . . . known as l'Avenue Hugh Cairns."

"A Great Tribute"

Commemoration plaque erected at Valenciennes

THE SECOND WORLD WAR

Dieppe Raid
From oil by C. F. Comfort. Canadian War Museum

OSBORN, John Robert

V.C.	Hong Kong, December 19th, 1941 (Posthumous)
Born	Norfolk, England, January 2nd, 1899
Unit	1st Battalion, The Winnipeg Grenadiers
Died	December 19th, 1941

A Company of the Winnipeg Grenadiers ... became divided during an attack on Mount Butler.... A part ... led by Company Sergeant-Major Osborn captured the hill at the point of the bayonet and held it for three hours when ... the position became untenable.... With no consideration for his own safety he assisted and directed stragglers to the new Company position exposing himself to heavy enemy fire to cover their retirement....

The Company was ... completely surrounded by the enemy who were able to approach to within grenade throwing distance of the slight depression which the Company were holding. Several enemy grenades were thrown which ... Osborn picked up and threw back. The enemy threw a grenade which landed in a position where it was impossible to pick it up and return it in time. Shouting a warning to his comrades this gallant Warrant Officer threw himself on the grenade which exploded killing him instantly.

Canada Gazette, April 6, 1946

[The British named a barracks after Osborn, at Hong Kong.]

John Robert Osborn

MERRITT, Charles Cecil Ingersoll

V.C.	Dieppe, August 19th, 1942
Born	Vancouver, November 10th, 1908
Unit	The South Saskatchewan Regiment
	Residing at Vancouver

The bridge was about 200 yards long, really a kind of causeway. It was wide and had no balustrades. That made it very exposed. On the hill across the river was a high concrete fort, its guns all trained on the bridge. The river was in flood and the bridge was the only way to get across apart from swimming.

I saw the first men try to cross. Great chunks of concrete flew in the air — mortar shells exploding. Bullets pinged off the road. In a minute or two, what had been a smooth concrete road was gashed with craters and pock-marked with bullet holes. Our men were mowed down.

Striding up the road unhurried, revolver dangling from his hip, came Lt. Col. Cecil Merritt, the Saskatchewans' CO. As he reached us he took his tin hat off and wiped sweat from his forehead. It was a hot, steamy day. He asked what the trouble was. Someone said: "This bridge is a hot spot, sir. We're trying to get across it."

"Now men," he said, "we're going to get across. Follow me. Don't bunch up together, spread out. Here we go!" Erect and bare-headed, he strode forward onto the bridge. His helmet hung from his wrist as he walked. As I watched him lead his men through that thundering barrage, I felt a quiver run up and down my spine. I'd never seen anything like it.

War correspondent Wallace Reyburn,
in a Canadian Broadcasting Corporation report

War poster. Canadian War Museum

After several of his runners became casualties he himself kept contact with his different positions. Although twice wounded, Lieutenant-Colonel Merritt continued to direct the unit's operations with great vigor and determination and while organizing the withdrawal he stalked a sniper with a Bren Gun and silenced him. He then coolly gave orders for the departure and announced his intention to hold off and "get even with" the enemy. . . .

Lt.-Col. Merritt is now reported to be a prisoner of war.

Canada Gazette, October 10, 1942

FOOTE, John Weir

V.C.	Dieppe, August 19th, 1942
Born	Madoc, Ontario, May 5th, 1904
Service	Canadian Chaplain Services, attached to The Royal Hamilton Light Infantry

Residing at Cobourg, Ontario

[The Reverend John Foote was the first member of the Canadian Chaplain Services ever to win the Victoria Cross.]

Gallantry was shown in no sudden blaze of violent action but coolly and calmly through eight hours of the gruelling, terrible battle of Dieppe, in which he "... exposed himself to an inferno of fire and saved many lives by his gallant efforts ... his example inspired all around him. Those who observed him state that the calmness of this heroic man as he walked about, collecting the wounded on the fireswept beach, will never be forgotten."

Then, at the end of his trial by fire, he climbed from the landing craft that was to have taken him to safety, and walked courageously into the German positions, that he might be taken prisoner and so minister to those men whose fate for the next three years was to be barbed wire and chains.

The Legionary, March, 1946

Foote, with his wife, in 1946

PETERS, Frederick Thornton

V.C.	Oran, North Africa, November 8th, 1942
Born	Charlottetown, Prince Edward Island, September 17th, 1889
Service	Royal Navy
Died	November 11th, 1943 (in an air crash off Gibraltar, on his way to England for the presentation of the award)

[H.M.S. *Walney* and H.M.S. *Hartland* were two ex-American coastguard ships that were lost in a gallant attempt to force the boom defences in the harbour of Oran during the landings on the North African coast.] Captain Peters led his force through the boom towards the jetty in the face of point-blank fire from shore batteries, a Destroyer and a Cruiser. Blinded in one eye, he alone of the seventeen Officers and Men on the bridge survived. The Walney reached the jetty disabled and ablaze, and went down with her colours flying.

London Gazette, May 18, 1943

Frederick Thornton Peters

TRIQUET, Paul

V.C.	Casa Berardi, Italy, December 14th, 1943
Born	Cabano, Quebec, April 2nd, 1910
Service	Royal 22e Régiment
	Residing at Limoilou, Quebec

The capture of the key road junction on the main Ortona–Orsogna lateral was entirely dependent on securing the hamlet of Casa Berardi. . . . Captain Triquet's company . . . with the support of a squadron of a Canadian armoured regiment, was given the task of crossing the gully and securing Casa Berardi. . . . The gully was held in strength and on approaching it the force came under heavy fire from machine guns and mortars. All the company officers and fifty per cent of the men were killed or wounded. Showing superb contempt for the enemy, Captain Triquet went round reorganizing the remainder and encouraging them with the words "Never mind them, they can't shoot. . . . There are enemy in front of us, behind us, and on our flanks, there is only one safe place, that is on the objective." . . . [He] dashed forward and with his men following him, broke through the enemy resistance. In this action four tanks were destroyed and several enemy machine gun posts silenced. . . .

Captain Triquet and his company, in close co-operation with the tanks, forced their way on until a position was reached on the outskirts of Casa Berardi. By this time the strength of the company was reduced to two sergeants and fifteen men. In expectation of a counter-attack, Captain Triquet at once set about organizing his handful of men into a defensive perimeter around the remaining tanks and passed the mot d'ordre "Ils ne passeront pas." A German counter-attack supported by tanks developed almost immediately. Captain Triquet . . . was everywhere encouraging his men and directing the defence, and by using whatever weapons were to hand personally accounted for several of the enemy. This and subsequent attacks were beaten off with heavy losses and Captain Triquet and his small force held out against overwhelming odds until the remainder of the battalion took Casa Berardi and relieved them the next day.

Canada Gazette, March 11, 1944

King George VI chats with Triquet in Italy

HOEY, Charles Ferguson

V.C.	Maungdaw, Burma, February 16th, 1944 (Posthumous)
Born	Duncan, B.C., March 29th, 1914
Unit	1st Battalion, The Lincolnshire Regiment (British Army)
Died	February 16th, 1944

[Canadian-born Charles Hoey joined the British Army in 1933. He was commissioned in 1936 and sailed for India with the Lincolns the following year. His battalion moved to Burma in 1942.]

In Burma . . . , 1944, Major Hoey's Company formed part of a force which was ordered to capture a position at all costs.

After a night march through enemy held territory the force was met at the foot of the position by heavy machine-gun fire.

Major Hoey personally led his Company under heavy machine-gun and rifle fire right up to the objective. Although wounded at least twice in the leg and head he seized a Bren gun from one of his men and firing from the hip, led his Company onto the objective. In spite of his wounds the Company had difficulty in keeping up with him, and Major Hoey reached the enemy strong post first where he killed all the occupants before being mortally wounded.

Major Hoey's outstanding gallantry and leadership, his total disregard of personal safety and his grim determination to reach the objective resulted in the capture of this vital position.

London Gazette, May 18, 1944

Charles Ferguson Hoey

MAHONY, John Keefer

V.C.   Melfa River, Italy, May 24th, 1944

Born   New Westminster, B.C., June 30th, 1911

Unit   The Westminster Regiment (Motor)

Residing at London, Ontario

[A company of the Westminster Regiment (Motor) under the command of Major Mahony received orders to establish the initial bridgehead across the river Melfa. Mahony personally led his company down to and across the river under heavy enemy fire.]

From 1530 hours the company maintained itself in the face of enemy fire and attack until 2030 hours when the remaining companies and supporting weapons were able to cross....

Early in the action Major Mahony was wounded in the head and twice in the leg, but he refused medical aid and continued to direct the defence.... The enemy perceived that this officer was the soul of the defence and consequently fired at him constantly with all weapons.

Canada Gazette, July 15, 1944

To the Westminsters, huddled in their narrow bridgehead, their numbers steadily diminishing under the fire which raked them continuously, and menaced at all times by the grim prospect of being overrun by armour, their company commander was a constant source of inspiration.... He was decorated by King George VI on 31 July, when His Majesty, travelling incognito as "General Collingwood," reviewed Canadian troops near Raviscanina in the Volturno Valley.

The Canadians in Italy

John Keefer Mahony

MYNARSKI, Andrew Charles

V.C.	Over Cambrai, June 12th, 1944 (Posthumous)
Born	Winnipeg, October 14th, 1916
Service	Royal Canadian Air Force
Died	June 12th, 1944

Pilot Officer Mynarski was the mid-upper gunner of a Lancaster aircraft detailed to attack a target at Cambrai in France, on the night of 12th June, 1944. The aircraft was attacked from below and astern by an enemy fighter.... Fire broke out ... and the captain ordered the crew to abandon the aircraft.... Mynarski left his turret and went towards the escape hatch. He then saw that the rear gunner was still in his turret and apparently unable to leave it....

Without hesitation ... Mynarski made his way through the flames in an endeavour to reach the rear turret and release the gunner. Whilst so doing, his parachute and his clothing, up to the waist, were set on fire. All his efforts to move the turret and free the gunner were in vain. Eventually the rear gunner clearly indicated to him that there was nothing more he could do and that he should try to save his own life. Pilot Officer Mynarski reluctantly went back through the flames to the escape hatch. There, as a last gesture to the trapped gunner, he turned towards him, stood to attention in his flaming clothes and saluted, before he jumped out of the aircraft.... He was found eventually by the French, but was so severely burnt that he died from his injuries.

London Gazette, October 11, 1946

[The rear gunner miraculously survived the crash.]

Andrew Charles Mynarski
Painting by Paul Goranson. Canadian War Museum

HORNELL, David Ernest

V.C.	Shetland Islands, June 24th, 1944 (Posthumous)
Born	Mimico, Ontario, January 26th, 1910
Service	Royal Canadian Air Force
Died	June 25th, 1944

Flight Lieutenant Hornell was captain and first air pilot of a twin-engined amphibian aircraft engaged on an anti-submarine patrol in northern waters. The patrol had lasted some hours when a fully-surfaced U-boat was sighted.... The U-boat opened up with anti-aircraft fire which became increasingly fierce and accurate.... He brought his aircraft down very low and released his depth charges in a perfect straddle. The bows of the U-boat were lifted out of the water; it sank and members of the crew were seen in the sea.

Flight Lieutenant Hornell contrived, by superhuman efforts at the controls, to gain a little height.... fire in the starboard wing had grown more intense and the vibration had increased. Then the burning engine fell off.... With the utmost coolness, the captain took his aircraft into the wind and, despite the manifold dangers, brought it safely down on the heavy swell. Badly damaged and blazing furiously, the aircraft rapidly settled.

After ordeal by fire came ordeal by water. There was only one serviceable dinghy and this could not hold all the crew. So they took turns in the water, holding on to the sides.... The survivors were finally rescued after they had been in the water for 21 hours. By this time ... Hornell was blinded and completely exhausted. He died shortly after being picked up.

London Gazette, July 28, 1944

RAF air-sea rescue launch approaches Hornell's dinghy

BAZALGETTE, Ian Willoughby

V.C.	Trossy St. Maximin, France, August 4th, 1944 (Posthumous)
Born	Calgary, October 19th, 1918
Service	Royal Air Force
Died	August 4th, 1944

Bazalgette was "master bomber" of a Pathfinder squadron detailed to mark an important target . . . for the main bomber force.

When nearing the target his Lancaster came under heavy anti-aircraft fire. Both starboard engines were put out of action and serious fires broke out. . . . The bomb aimer was badly wounded.

As the deputy "master bomber" had already been shot down, the success of the attack depended on Squadron Leader Bazalgette and this he knew. Despite the appalling conditions in his burning aircraft, he pressed on gallantly to the target, marking and bombing it accurately. . . .

After the bombs had been dropped the Lancaster dived, practically out of control. By expert airmanship and great exertion . . . Bazalgette regained control. But the port inner engine then failed and the whole of the starboard main-plane became a mass of flames. . . .

Bazalgette fought bravely to bring his aircraft and crew to safety. The mid-upper gunner was overcome by fumes. Squadron Leader Bazalgette ordered those of his crew who were able to leave by parachute to do so. He remained at the controls and attempted the almost hopeless task of landing the crippled and blazing aircraft in a last effort to save the wounded bomb aimer and helpless air gunner. With superb skill, and taking great care to avoid a small French village nearby, he brought the aircraft down safely. Unfortunately it then exploded and this gallant officer and his two comrades perished.

London Gazette, August 17, 1945

Ian Willoughby Bazalgette

CURRIE, David Vivian

V.C.	St. Lambert-sur-Dives, France, August 18th, 1944
Born	Sutherland, Saskatchewan, July 8th, 1912
Unit	29th Armoured Reconnaissance Regiment (The South Alberta Regiment)

Residing at Ottawa

"Germans surrendering to Major D. V. Currie's force. Major Currie himself, tired and grimy, appears at the left, pistol in hand. This is as close as we are ever likely to come to a photograph of a man winning the Victoria Cross." – C. P. Stacey, *The Victory Campaign*

Major Currie first attacked and seized the village [St. Lambert-sur-Dives] which was a key point of the Chambois–Trun escape route for the remnants of two German armies cut off in the Falaise pocket. He held it through three days and nights of continuous fighting hurling back repeated enemy attempts to force a breakthrough. His strategy was successful in blocking the German escape route.... [He] took his tiny force of tanks, anti-tank guns and infantry and thrust them in the path of vastly superior forces and firepower....

When two of his tanks were knocked out he went on foot through many enemy outposts successfully to extricate the crews of his disabled tanks....

Says the citation:

"Throughout the operations the casualties to Major Currie's force were heavy. However, he never considered the possibility of failure or allowed it to enter the minds of his men. In the words of one of his non-commissioned officers, 'We knew at one stage that it was going to be a fight to the finish, but he was so cool about it, it was impossible for us to get excited.'"

In a final assault, Major Currie's little band destroyed seven enemy tanks, twelve 88-millimeter guns and 40 vehicles, killed 300 Germans, wounded 500 and captured 1100 more. He then ordered an attack and completed the capture of the village.

The Legionary, January 1945

SMITH, Ernest Alvia

V.C.	Savio River, Italy, October 21st-22nd, 1944
Born	New Westminster, B.C., May 3rd, 1914
Unit	The Seaforth Highlanders of Canada
	Residing at New Westminster

Projector, Infantry, Anti-Tank (PIAT), at the Canadian War Museum

Ernest Alvia Smith

The action which followed is a striking demonstration of what may be accomplished by well-trained and determined infantry in the face of armoured attack, and is illumined by the gallantry of a member of the Seaforth's tank-hunting platoon — Private E. A. Smith. 'C' Company was already under fire from the approaching enemy tanks as Pte. Smith led his PIAT team across an open field to a roadside ditch, which offered the close range he needed. Almost at once a Mark V came lumbering down the road, sweeping the ditches with its machine-guns, and wounding Smith's companion. At a range of only 30 feet, and exposed to the full view of the enemy, Pte. Smith fired his PIAT. The bomb stopped the Panther, and its driver made frantic but futile efforts to turn around and retreat. Immediately ten German infantrymen tumbled off the back of the tank and charged Smith with machine pistols and grenades. Without hesitation he moved into the centre of the road, shot down four of them with his tommy gun, and dispersed the remainder. A second tank now opened fire from a safe distance and more Grenadiers began closing in on Smith. But the intrepid Highlander met this second threat just as steadfastly. Replenishing his ammunition from his wounded comrade in the ditch he continued to protect him, fighting off the enemy with his sub-machine gun until they gave up and withdrew in disorder.

The Canadians in Italy

COSENS, Aubrey

V.C.	Mooshof, Germany, February 25th-26th, 1945 (Posthumous)
Born	Latchford, Ontario, May 21st, 1921
Unit	The Queen's Own Rifles of Canada
Died	February 26th, 1945

On the 3rd Division's front [during the Rhineland fighting], The Queen's Own Rifles of Canada were having a difficult time.... The enemy had converted three farm buildings into strongpoints, and from these the leading platoon was twice driven back.... A German counter-attack was beaten off in bitter, confused fighting at a cost of many casualties, including the platoon officer.

In this emergency Sergeant Aubrey Cosens took command of the other survivors of his platoon, only four in number.

The Victory Campaign

"I'm going to get a Hussar tank to bust its way through the wall on this side of the main farmhouse," he said. "I'll go through the hole and take the Jerries in the rear. Cover me until I get to the tank. When I run to the house, I want you to give me plenty of covering fire. If you can keep them busy they might not see what's happening."

The four riflemen kept up a fusillade of shots at the windows of the farmhouse as Cosens sprinted across the open field to the nearest tank.... From the back of the turret of a Sherman tank, Cosens was seen coolly directing its fire on the house. In a few minutes the tank roared forward and took up a hull-down position closer to the buildings firing high-explosive ammunition with its 75-mm. gun.

At this moment Sgt. Cosens appeared again, racing forward on foot. He disappeared behind a fold in the ground and, making use of cover, was soon within assaulting distance of the house. He seemed to lead a charmed life. The desperate German riflemen did their best to gun him down. While he was attracting their attention the Sherman tank suddenly emerged from cover and, racing like a juggernaut for the farmhouse, crashed through the wall.

While the bricks were still falling, Cosens plunged forward and disappeared through the hole.

The four riflemen, meanwhile, continued to engage the enemy. Inside, the Sergeant was shooting his way from room to room, killing or wounding the surprised occupants.

After clearing the main farmhouse of the enemy, Cosens charged the second and third buildings alone, routing the defenders despite a hail of machine gun and small arms slugs. A number of dazed enemy gave themselves up to the terrible figure who apparently was invulnerable to point-blank fire....

He was on his way to report to his company commander when he was shot through the head by an enemy sniper. He died instantly. He was only 23.

The Legionary

The bronze plaque being unveiled by an officer of the Queen's Own marks the place where Aubrey Cosens won the Victoria Cross.

TILSTON, Frederick Albert

V.C.	The Hochwald, Germany, March 1st, 1945
Born	Toronto, June 11th, 1906
Unit	The Essex Scottish Regiment
	Residing at Aurora, Ontario

On the western edge of the Hochwald one man epitomizes the spirit which finally won the forest and the route across the Rhine. He is Freddie Tilston, the man who "never would make an officer."

It's his first attack as a company commander and his last. Across 500 yards of open ground with no tank support, Major Tilston leads his company just behind the creeping barrage. He is wounded, for the first time, in the head. Into enemy trenches he charges, firing his Sten from the hip. His left platoon comes under heavy fire. He dashes forward and silences the machine gun with a grenade.

He approaches the wood. Flying steel smashes into his hip and he falls. He waves his men on, then struggles to his feet and catches up.

His wounds are forgotten as he leads the sadly depleted company into hand to hand fighting with the enemy....

Fred Tilston consolidates his position ... then stumbles from platoon to platoon urging his men to hold the vicious counter-attacks which slash into grenade-throwing distance.

His ammunition runs low and ... [Tilston] crosses the bullet-swept ground to the company on the left to replenish the supply of grenades and bullets. Six times he lurches across the deadly killing ground; but this was no ordinary man the enemy soldiers squinted at through their sights. He just couldn't be killed or stopped.

But on his last trip he is hit again, in the other leg. This time he stays on the ground.... His concern was not for his shattered legs, but only to pass on the plan and to urge his men to hold.

And as medical assistance finally came, his only words were: "We held."

The Legionary, March, 1955

Frederick Albert Tilston

TOPHAM, Frederick George

V.C.	East of the Rhine, March 24th, 1945
Born	Toronto, August 10th, 1917
Unit	1st Canadian Parachute Battalion
	Residing at Weston, Ontario

[Corporal Topham, a medical orderly, parachuted with his battalion on to a strongly defended area east of the Rhine.]

During this fighting ... Topham won the fourth Victoria Cross awarded to a Canadian during the campaign. As he treated casualties after the drop, Topham heard a cry for help from a wounded man in the open. The recommendation for the decoration continues:

"Two medical orderlies from a field ambulance went out to this man in succession but both were killed as they knelt beside the casualty. Without hesitation and on his own initiative Corporal Topham went forward through intense fire to replace the orderlies who had been killed before his eyes. As he worked on the wounded man, he was himself shot through the nose. In spite of severe bleeding and intense pain he never faltered in his task. Having completed immediate first aid, he carried the wounded man steadily and slowly back through continuous fire to the shelter of the woods."

Refusing assistance for his own wound, he continued to perform his duties for two hours, until all casualties had been evacuated from the area. Then, having successfully resisted orders for his own removal, he rescued three men from a burning carrier at great risk from exploding ammunition. His heroic conduct serves to emphasize the great debt owed by the Army to its medical services.

The Victory Campaign

Frederick George Topham

GRAY, Robert Hampton

V.C.	Onagawa Wan, Japan, August 9th, 1945 (Posthumous)
Born	Trail, B.C., November 2nd, 1917
Service	Royal Canadian Naval Volunteer Reserve (attached to the Fleet Air Arm of the Royal Navy)
Died	August 9th, 1945

On August 9 — the day the A-bomb was dropped on Nagasaki — the Corsairs roared off again for Japan. As they approached Onagawa Wan, smudges of flak told the pilots it would be a difficult target.

Fire from the enemy anti-aircraft guns was intense as the Corsairs peeled off to attack warships in the bay. Gray drew a bead on a destroyer and swung onto an attacking course. His aircraft was immediately coned by fire from ship and shore. Shells and tracer ripped the diving aircraft. Flame and smoke plumed out behind. But Gray held his course. As the plane dived closer through the punishing flak, Gray's wingmates sensed what was happening.

It was a matter of split-seconds and courage now. Would the plane hold together long enough? The wounded Corsair screamed to within 150 feet of the destroyer ... 100 feet ... 75 feet ... Gray was now beyond the limits of ordinary courage. He could have dropped his bombs from a safer height and preserved a bit of precious altitude.

Even with a badly damaged aircraft, at some point on the run he made his decision. If he released his bombs and pulled up, he might make it back to the carrier. At worst, it would probably mean a ditching. But he didn't pull up. He dived to within 50 feet of the enemy destroyer before dropping his bombs. One struck directly amid-ships. A second bomb either hit the target or exploded ... alongside. The destroyer sank almost immediately.

"Valour Unlimited"

Corsairs over Onagawa Wan

PART II

GEORGE CROSS WINNERS

The George Cross

WAV/3

MINISTRY OF DEFENCE
Adastral House, Theobalds Road, LONDON W.C.1
Telephone: HOLborn 3434, ext.

AIR MAIL

Please address any reply to
MINISTRY OF DEFENCE
(S10j(Air))

and quote: AF/7144/70/II/S10j(Air)
Your reference: MMB47

The Chief Curator
Canadian War Museum
330 Sussex Drive
Ottawa
Ontario K1A OM8
Canada   17 August 1971

THE LATE AC1 FROST E R C

Reference is made to your letter of 28 July 1971, which
has been passed to this Department for reply. The
information you requested is as follows:

(1) The date and place of the Deed was 12 March 1940
     90 Squadron, West Raynham.

(2) Initial Award Empire Gallantry Medal
     converted to the George Cross on 24 September 1940.

(3) Presented with the award on 21 October 1940.

M.I.A. Owen

FROST, Ernest Ralph Clyde

G.C.	R.A.F. Station, West Raynham, England March 12th, 1940
Born	Three Rivers, Quebec, July 22nd, 1917
Service	Royal Air Force and Royal Canadian Air Force
Died	Sarnia, Ontario, July 28th, 1969

Two Leading Aircraftmen of the RAF, Michael Campion and Ernest Clyde Frost, displayed great courage when two Blenheim aircraft collided whilst taking off. At great risk to themselves they managed to rescue the unconscious pilot of one aircraft from the burning wreckage. Shortly afterwards the tanks exploded and the whole aircraft was rapidly burnt out. Unfortunately the pilot died later.

The Story of the George Cross

[Both men were decorated for their gallantry.]

Ernest Ralph Clyde Frost

PATTON, John MacMillan Stevenson

G.C.	Weybridge, Surrey, England, September 21st, 1940
Born	Warwick, Bermuda, August 29th, 1915
Unit	1st Battalion, Royal Canadian Engineers
	Residing at Hamilton, Bermuda

On 21st September, as a result of a daylight raid, an unexploded bomb was left on the surface in the nearby Hawker Hurricane works. Hearing of a request for help Patton went quickly to the site and skidded the bomb on to a sheet of corrugated iron.... The bomb was then drawn clear and into a convenient field where it was dumped into an existing crater. It exploded some hours later. Patton's knowledge of German bombs, like that of all Canadians at the time, was of the slightest and, had the bomb exploded in the factory, it would certainly have slowed most essential production.

History of the Corps of Royal Canadian Engineers

Patton (left) after the investiture

HENDRY, James

G.C.	Loch Laggan, Scotland, June 13th, 1941 (Posthumous)
Born	Falkirk, Scotland, December 20th, 1911
Unit	No. 1 Tunnelling Company, RCE
Died	June 13th, 1941

[During 1941, a company of the Royal Canadian Engineers constructed a tunnel in Scotland.]

On 13th June . . . disaster struck. At about 1600 hours, Corporal James Hendry came out of the tunnel to find the powder house on fire. Shouting an alarm he ran to warn the compressor man and the steel-sharpener in the workshop, both unaware of the blaze though close by, and picking up a pail of water he headed for the powder house to try to put the fire out. Although he could easily have gotten clear, others nearby were also in danger, and if the magazine blew up, the resulting damage would put a stop to the job for some time. He was an experienced miner and fully aware of the chance he took. The gallant attempt failed; there was a devastating explosion in which Hendry died. Hoist house, workshop and powder house disappeared. The steel-sharpening shop was flattened and caught fire. A number of men were hurt, two seriously, and one was killed by a falling stone as he emerged from the tunnel. However the timely warning had enabled others to take cover and had prevented a much worse disaster.

History of the Corps of Royal Canadian Engineers

In this snapshot, Hendry appears on the right

GRAVELL, Karl Mander

G.C.	Simons Valley, Alberta, November 10th, 1941 (Posthumous)
Born	Norrköping, Sweden, September 27th, 1922
Service	Royal Canadian Air Force
Died	November 10th, 1941

The ... George Cross was received by Leading Aircraftman K. M. Gravell, who joined the RCAF on 15 March 1941 as a nineteen year old high school student in his home town, Vancouver. L.A.C. Gravell's heart was set on becoming a wireless operator/air gunner so, after completing manning depot training, he was sent to No. 2 Wireless School at Calgary.

He finished his groundschool subjects then began his flying training. On 10 November 1941 he took off on a routine training flight in a Tiger Moth with his pilot, F/O J. Robinson. When the exercise was completed the aircraft headed back to base. For some reason, that will never be determined, the Tiger Moth plunged into Simons Valley and burst into flames. L.A.C. Gravell was severely injured. He lost one eye and suffered burns but he managed to get clear of the aircraft.

When he realized that his pilot was still in the burning wreckage he started back, ignoring the fact that his clothing was ablaze. A school teacher, Mrs. F. Walsh, who was subsequently awarded the George Medal for her action, ran up to L.A.C. Gravell and dragged him away. She rolled him on the ground to extinguish the flames which had, by this time, completely enveloped his clothing.

L.A.C. Gravell subsequently died from his burns. Had he not considered his pilot before his own safety and had immediately extinguished the flames on his clothing, he would probably not have lost his life.

Karl Mander Gravell

The Dangerous Sky

BASTIAN, Gordon Love

*G.C.	500 miles off Brest, France, March 30th, 1943
Born	Barry, Wales, March 30th, 1902. First came to Canada in 1927.
Service	Merchant Navy (British)
	Residing at Montreal

The ship in which Mr. Bastian was serving was torpedoed and sustained severe damage. Mr. Bastian was on watch in the engine-room when the ship was struck. He at once shut off the engines. He then remembered that two firemen were on watch in the stokehold. The engine-room was in darkness and water was already pouring into it. Although there was grave risk of disastrous flooding in opening the watertight door between the stokehold and engine-room, Mr. Bastian did not hesitate but groped his way to the door and opened it. The two firemen were swept into the engine-room with the inrush of water. One man had a broken arm and injured feet and the other was badly bruised and shaken. Mr. Bastian made efforts to hold them both but lost one, so he dragged the other to the escape ladder and helped him on deck. He then returned for the other and helped him to safety. The more seriously injured man had practically to be lifted up the ladder by Mr. Bastian, who was himself half choked by cordite fumes.

Second Engineer Officer Bastian took a very great risk in opening the watertight door into the already flooded and darkened engine-room of the sinking ship and both men undoubtedly owe their lives to his exceptional bravery, strength and presence of mind.

London Gazette, August 17, 1943

Gordon Love Bastian
Painting by Bernard Hailstone. Imperial War Museum

*The original award of the Albert Medal was later converted to the George Cross

SPOONER, Kenneth Gerald

G.C.	Over Lake Erie, May 14th, 1943 (Posthumous)
Born	Smiths Falls, Ontario, May 24th, 1922
Service	Royal Canadian Air Force
Died	May 14th, 1943

This airman, a student Navigator with no pilot training, displayed great courage, resolution and unselfishness in the face of harassing circumstances when the pilot of the aircraft fainted at the controls. While other crew members were vainly trying to remove him from his seat he temporarily regained consciousness and froze on the controls causing the aircraft to lose altitude rapidly. Immediately after the pilot became indisposed, L.A.C. Spooner, with extreme coolness and courage assumed charge, ordered the remainder of the crew to bail out while he took over the controls and endeavoured to keep the aircraft at a safe height. Three members of the crew bailed out as instructed and shortly after the aircraft crashed carrying the unconscious pilot and L.A.C. Spooner to their death. The crash occurred approximately one hour after the pilot had lost control. This airman, with complete disregard for his personal safety and in conformity with the highest tradition of the Service sacrificed his life in order to save the lives of his comrades.

Canada Gazette, January 1, 1944

Kenneth Gerald Spooner

RENNIE, John

G.C.	Slough, England, October 29th, 1943 (Posthumous)
Born	Aberdeen, Scotland, December 13th, 1920
Service	The Argyll and Sutherland Highlanders of Canada
Died	October 29th, 1943

[For conspicuous courage in the face of extreme danger on the 29th October, 1943.]

Acting Sergeant Rennie was supervising grenade throwing by a member of his unit at a Canadian Training Camp in England. One grenade had been successfully thrown but a second grenade failed to clear the protective embankment, and rolled back into the throwing area.

Despite the fact that he had the time and opportunity to escape from danger ... Rennie without the slightest hesitation dashed forward, interposing himself between the grenade and his comrades, and attempted to pick up the rolling grenade and throw it clear. Before he could do so, however, the grenade exploded and Acting Sergeant Rennie sustained mortal injuries.

By his sacrifice ... Rennie prevented serious and possibly fatal injuries to three other soldiers who were within five yards of the explosion and his gallant act, carried out in complete disregard of his own safety, showed bravery of a high order that stands out in the annals of the Canadian Army.

London Gazette, May 27, 1944

John Rennie

ROSS, Arthur Dwight

G.C.	R.A.F. Station Tholthorpe, Yorkshire, England, June 28th, 1944
Born	Winnipeg, March 18th, 1907
Service	Royal Canadian Air Force
	Residing at Kingston, Ontario

[Air Commodore Ross] was about to enter the debriefing room [when] there was a great yellow flash on the airfield. Running to the scene Ross found that an Alouette Squadron aircraft, returning from the operation on three engines, had crashed into another aircraft . . . loaded with bombs. By the time he arrived both aircraft were burning fiercely with gas tanks and bombs in imminent danger of exploding.

A/C Ross immediately took charge, assisted by Flight Sergeant J. R. St. Germain, the bomb aimer of another aircraft, Corporal M. Marquet and Leading Aircraftmen M. M. McKenzie and R. R. Wolfe. A/C Ross and Marquet had just extricated the pilot when ten 500-pound bombs exploded. The rescuers were hurled to the ground. Undeterred by the flames which were now rapidly approaching the tail, the Air Commodore, assisted by St. Germain, McKenzie and Wolfe turned his attention to the imprisoned rear gunner of the Alouette. . . . Finally St. Germain and Marquet had to break the steel supports of the turret to extricate the gunner. Just then another bomb explosion threw the rescuers to the ground again. St. Germain, rising quickly, covered one of the victims with his own body to protect him. The Air Commodore was struck by flying debris and lost his right hand.

Ross leads Air Marshal L. S. Breadner from the room he was about to enter nine days later when the crash occurred.

Turning the further rescues over to his assistants Ross walked to the ambulance. . . . In the meantime Marquet, seeing that the burning petrol endangered two aircraft, supervised their removal while McKenzie and Wolfe continued their efforts to extinguish the fire. The entire crew of the Alouette aircraft was saved. Of the rescuers, McKenzie and Wolfe were injured as well as Ross. For their deeds in this incident St. Germain and Marquet received the George Medal. McKenzie and Wolfe were awarded the British Empire Medal.

The Dangerous Sky

GRAY, Roderick Borden

G.C.	Atlantic Ocean, August 27th, 1944 (Posthumous)
Born	Sault Ste. Marie, Ontario, October 2nd, 1917
Service	Royal Canadian Air Force
Died	August 27th-28th, 1944

[Flying Officer Gray was the navigator of a Coastal Command Wellington bomber that had spotted a German U-boat in the Atlantic. The bomber attacked, straddled the submarine with depth charges, but was itself set on fire by gunfire and crashed into the sea. Two of the crew were trapped in the aircraft but Gray and three others managed to extricate themselves. A survivor, Warrant Officer Gordon S. Bulley, reports:]

When I got to the surface I saw Cy [Gray] had managed to escape with a dinghy only large enough to hold one man. . . . Then we . . . heard the skipper calling for help. . . . He had been badly wounded. He couldn't move his right side. His left hand was badly smashed and his face was cut. Cy was also seriously injured and he told us he was sure his leg had been broken. For my own part I was quite OK. . . .

Not long after we got the skipper into the dinghy we heard cries for help coming from the other air gunner, F/Sgt. Ford. Cy and I both swam around and finally located him in the darkness. He had a broken arm and could not swim. We hauled him into the dinghy and put him on top of the skipper. . . . Cy and I clung to the dinghy until dawn. . . .

[Gray's companions begged him to get in but he refused. Knowing that the dinghy was already overloaded, he remained in the water clinging to the side.]

When dawn finally broke Cy showed no sign of life. We tried to shake him and immediately realized he was dead. There was nothing for us to do but cut him loose from the dinghy.

[During the afternoon a Sunderland flying boat rescued the three survivors.]

The Legionary, May, 1945

Photograph of the survivors, taken from the air.

PART III

VICTORIA AND GEORGE CROSS WINNERS ASSOCIATED WITH CANADA

VICTORIA CROSS WINNERS

PEARSON, John

V.C.	Gwalior, June 17th, 1858 (Indian Mutiny)
Born	Yorkshire, England, 1825
Unit	8th King's Royal Irish Hussars (British Army)
Died	Lion's Head, Ontario, April 18th, 1892, after residing in Canada for 12 years

RICHARDSON, George

V.C.	Kewarie Trans-Gogra, April 27th, 1859 (Indian Mutiny)
Born	Daralanna, Ireland, August 1st, 1831
Unit	34th (Cumberland) Regiment of Foot (British Army)
Died	London, Ontario, January 28th, 1923, after residing in Canada for 61 years

O'HEA, Timothy

V.C.	Danville, Quebec, June 9th, 1866. Award made for gallant conduct in extinguishing a fire in a railway ammunition car; it was the only V.C. ever won in Canada
Born	Bantry, County Cork, Ireland
Unit	The Rifle Brigade (British Army)
Died	November, 1874

NICKERSON, William Henry Snyder

V.C.	Wakkerstroom, South Africa, April 20th, 1900
Born	Saint John, New Brunswick, March 27th, 1875 (Father British Army chaplain serving in Canada)
Service	Royal Army Medical Corps
Died	Britain, April 10th, 1954

BEET, Barry Churchill

V.C.	Wakkerstroom, South Africa, April 22nd, 1900
Born	Brackendale Farm, Bingham, Nottinghamshire, England, April 1st, 1873
Unit	The Sherwood Foresters (Derbyshire Regiment) (British Army)
Died	Vancouver, January 10th, 1946, after residing in Canada for 40 years

ROBSON, Henry Howey

V.C.	Mount Kemmel, France, December 14th, 1914
Born	South Shields, Durham, England
Unit	The Royal Scots (British Army)
Died	Toronto, March 2nd, 1964, after residing in Canada for 45 years

GEARY, Benjamin Handley

V.C.	Hill 60, near Ypres, Belgium, April 20th-21st, 1915
Born	London, England, June 29th, 1891
Unit	The East Surrey Regiment (British Army)
	Resident in Canada since 1928

TOMBS, Joseph

V.C.	Near Rue du Bois, France, June 16th, 1915
Born	Birmingham, England, March 23rd, 1887
Unit	The King's (Liverpool Regiment) (British Army)
Died	Toronto, June 28th, 1966, after residing in Canada for 47 years

WILKINSON, Thomas Orde Lawder

V.C.	La Boiselle, France, July 5th, 1916 (Posthumous)
Born	Bridgenorth, Shropshire, England, June 29th, 1894. Emigrated to Canada in 1912
Unit	The Loyal North Lancashire Regiment (British Army)
Died	July 5th, 1916

RYDER, Robert

V.C.	Thiepval, France, September 26th-October 23rd, 1916
Born	Enfield, Middlesex, England
Unit	The Duke of Cambridge's Own (Middlesex Regiment) (British Army)
	Lived in New Brunswick but returned to England where he still resides

STUART, Ronald Neil

V.C.	At sea in H.M.S. *Pargust*, June 7th, 1917
Born	Liverpool, England. Father a member of an old Prince Edward Island family. Lived for some years in Montreal
Service	Royal Naval Reserve
Died	In England, February 8th, 1954

TRAIN, Charles William

V.C.	Palestine, December 8th, 1917
Born	London, England, September 21st, 1890
Unit	The London Regiment (London Scottish) (British Army)
Died	Vancouver, March 28th, 1965, after residing in Canada for 39 years

CRUICKSHANK, Robert Edward

V.C.	Middle East, May 1st, 1918
Born	Winnipeg, June 17th, 1888
Unit	The London Regiment (London Scottish) (British Army)
Died	In England, September 1st, 1961

GEORGE CROSS WINNERS

DAVIES, Robert

G.C.	London, England (St. Paul's Cathedral), September 12th, 1940. For bomb disposal; one of the three first recipients
Born	Cornwall, England, October 3rd, 1900
Service	Emigrated to Canada and joined Canadian Army January 11th, 1918. Remained in Canada between the wars. Joined Royal Engineers, March 6th, 1940

Believed to be living in Australia

BUTSON, Arthur Richard Cecil

*G.C.	Grahamland, Antarctica, July 27th, 1947
Born	Hankow, China, October 24th, 1922. Came to Canada in 1952.
	Residing at Hamilton, Ontario

[A member of the Royal Army Medical Corps, Doctor Butson joined the Falkland Islands Dependencies Survey and accompanied a British expedition to the Antarctic.]

On the evening of 26th July, 1947, an American member of the ... Expedition fell into a crevasse some 6 miles from Base. Two teams were sent to the rescue but the hazards of crossing a heavily crevassed glacier were much increased by darkness and it was not until 4 o'clock on the morning of 27th July that the crevasse into which the American had fallen was located. Butson immediately volunteered to be lowered into the crevasse where he found the American tightly wedged 106 feet down and suffering from shock and exhaustion. For nearly an hour he had to chip the ice away in an extremely confined space in order to free the American.... Butson then rendered the necessary medical aid.

London Gazette

In trying to free his pelvis and legs which were wedged in the lower narrower part of the crack I had to lie tilted head down and got stuck myself several times. At this point there was a booming noise and some loud cracks and several billion tons of ice were on the move. I could feel the crevasse narrow about half an inch on either side of my chest. I managed to extricate myself from this position and realized that there was some urgency in completing the job. Peterson appeared to have no serious injuries so I passed a rope sling under his thigh and got the men above to pull. After several attempts to pull him out, Peterson suddenly became dislodged and shot upwards. The rope was lowered again and the equipment hauled up, followed by myself. Peterson was placed in a tent and on examining him more carefully was found miraculously to have suffered only bruises and minor lacerations.

Extract from Dr. Butson's account,
Canadian War Museum

The Rescue Party

*The original award of the Albert Medal was later converted to the George Cross

INDEX

ALGIE, Wallace Lloyd 159
    D. J. Corrigall, *The History of the Twentieth Canadian Battalion (Central Ontario Regiment)*, Toronto, Regimental Association, 1935.
    Illustration: *War Illustrated Album de Luxe,* vol. ix.

BARKER, William George 163
    Frank McGuire, "Major Barker and His Sopwith Snipe," *Organization of Military Museums of Canada Bulletin*, vol. 1, No. 1, 1972.

BARRON, Colin Fraser 89
    D. J. Goodspeed, *Battle Royal, A History of the Royal Regiment of Canada, 1862-1962*, Toronto Regimental Association, 1962.
    Illustration: *War Illustrated Album de Luxe*, vol. ix.

BASTIAN, Gordon Love 211
BAZALGETTE, Ian Willoughby 187
    Photo: Public Archives of Canada.
BEET, Barry Churchill 223
BELLEW, Edward Donald 35
    Photo: Original with Princess Patricia's Canadian Light Infantry.
BENT, Philip Eric 73
    Illustration: *War Illustrated Album de Luxe*, vol. ix.
BISHOP, William Avery 59
BOURKE, Rowland Richard Louis 103
    Illustration: *The Sphere*, January 1st, 1918.
BRERETON, Alexander Picton 117
    Illustration: *War Illustrated Album de Luxe*, vol. vi.
BRILLANT, Jean 113
    J. Chaballe, *Histoire du 22e Bataillon canadien-français*, vol. 1, Montreal Regimental Association, 1952.
    Photo: *The Legionary*, Aug. 1971.
BROWN, Harry 61
    G. W. L. Nicholson, *Canadian Expeditionary Force, 1914-1918*, Ottawa, Queen's Printer, 1962.
    Illustration: *Times History of the War*, vol. xiii.
BUTSON, Arthur Richard Cecil 227
    Photo: Courtesy A. R. C. Butson.
CAIRNS, Hugh 165
    "A Great Tribute," *The Legionary*, June, 1936.
    Photo: Royal Canadian Legion photograph.
CAMPBELL, Frederick William 39
    Thirty Canadian V.Cs., London, Canadian War Records Office, n.d.
    Illustration from *Times History of the War*, vol. v.
CLARKE, Leo 41
    W. W. Murray, *The History of the 2nd Canadian Battalion (Eastern Ontario Regiment)*, Ottawa, Regimental Association, 1947
    The Times History of the War, vol. xii.
    Photo: Public Archives of Canada.

CLARK-KENNEDY, William Hew 129
    R. C. Fetherstonhaugh, *The 24th Battalion C.E.F., Victoria Rifles of Canada, 1914-1919*, Montreal, Gazette Printing Co., 1930.
    Photo: Public Archives of Canada.

COCKBURN, Hampden Zane Churchill 21
    G. O'M. Creagh and E. M. Humphris, *The Victoria Cross*, vol. I of *The V.C. and D.S.O.*, London, Standard Art Book Co., n.d.

COMBE, Robert Grierson 57
    G. O'M. Creagh and E. M. Humphris, *The Victoria Cross*, vol. I of *The V.C. and D.S.O.*, London, Standard Art Book Co., n.d.
    Photo: Public Archives of Canada.

COPPINS, Frederick George 119
    The Times History of the War, vol. xvii.
    Photo: *The Legionary*, November, 1965.

COSENS, Aubrey 193
    C. P. Stacey, *The Victory Campaign*, Ottawa, Queen's Printer, 1969.
    H. K. MacDonald, "The Legend of Aubrey Cosens, V.C.," *The Legionary*, February, 1964.
    Photo: Royal Canadian Legion.

CROAK, John Bernard 107
    The Times History of the War, vol. xvii.
    Photo: Public Archives of Canada.

CRUICKSHANK, Robert Edward 225
CURRIE, David Vivian 189
    "Canada's Seventh V.C.," *The Legionary*, January, 1945.
    Photo: C. P. Stacey, *The Victory Campaign*, Ottawa, Queen's Printer, 1960.

DAVIES, Robert 225
De WIND, Edmund 95
    C. I. Foster, ed., *Letters from the Front . . .* , Toronto, Canadian Bank of Commerce, 1920.
    Photo: from *Letters from the Front*.

DINESEN, Thomas 123
    C. Beresford Topp, *The 42nd Battalion, C.E.F. Royal Highlanders of Canada . . .* , Montreal, Gazette Printing Co., 1931.
    Photo: Public Archives of Canada.

DOUGLAS, Campbell Mellis 15
    P. A. Wilkins, *The History of the Victoria Cross*, London, A. Constable & Co., 1904.
    Photo: Public Archives of Canada.

DUNN, Alexander Roberts 5
    Richard Brett-Smith, *The 11th Hussars*, London, Leo Cooper Ltd., 1969.
    Photo: Public Archives of Canada.

FISHER, Fred 31
    R. C. Fetherstonhaugh, ed., *The 13th Battalion Royal*

Highlanders of Canada, Montreal, Regimental Association, 1925.

FLOWERDEW, Gordon Muriel — 99
Thirty Canadian V.Cs., London, Canadian War Records Office, n.d.

FOOTE, John Weir — 173
Photo: Royal Canadian Legion.

FROST, Ernest Ralph Clyde — 203
J. Smyth, *The Story of the George Cross*, London, Arthur Barker Ltd., 1968.
Photo: Public Archives of Canada.

GEARY, Benjamin Handley — 223

GOOD, Herman James — 109
R. C. Fetherstonhaugh, ed., *The 13th Battalion Royal Highlanders of Canada*, Montreal, Regimental Association, 1925.
Photo: Courtesy, Herman J. Good V.C., Branch No. 18, Royal Canadian Legion.

GRAVELL, Karl Mander — 209
Tom Coughlin, *The Dangerous Sky*, Toronto, Ryerson, 1968.
Photo: Public Archives of Canada.

GRAY, Robert Hampton — 199
Norman Shannon, "Valour Unlimited," *Legion*, November, 1969.
Photo: Public Archives of Canada.

GRAY, Roderick Borden — 219
Warrant Officer Gordon S. Bulley, quoted in "A George Cross Hero," *The Legionary*, May 1945.

GREGG, Milton Fowler — 151
R. C. Featherstonhaugh, *The Royal Canadian Regiment, 1883-1933*, Montreal, Gazette Printing Co., 1936.
Photo: *Times History of the War*, vol. xix.

HALL, Frederick William — 33
Thirty Canadian V.Cs., London, Canadian War Records Office, n.d.
Illustration: *War Illustrated Album de Luxe*, vol. vii, London, Amalgamated Press.

HALL, William — 11
John Hundevad, "Man of Valour," *The Legionary*, April, 1968.
Photo: Public Archives of Canada.

HANNA, Robert — 69
Photo: Public Archives of Canada.

HARVEY, Frederick Maurice Watson — 47
G. O'M. Creagh and E. M. Humphris, *The Victoria Cross*, vol. I of *The V.C. and D.S.O.*, London, Standard Art Book Co., n.d.
Photo: Public Archives of Canada.

HENDRY, James — 207
A. J. Kerry and W. A. McDill, *The History of The Corps of Royal Canadian Engineers*, vol. I, Ottawa, Military Engineers Association, 1962.
Photo: Public Archives of Canada.

HOBSON, Frederick — 65
D. J. Corrigall, *The History of the Twentieth Canadian Battalion (Central Ontario Regiment)*, Toronto, Regimental Association, 1935.
Illustration: *War Illustrated Album de Luxe*, vol. ix, London, Amalgamated Press.

HOEY, Charles Ferguson   179
Photo: Public Archives of Canada.
HOLLAND, Edward James Gibson   25

HOLMES, Thomas William   75
Thirty Canadian V.Cs., London, Canadian War Records Office, n.d.
Photo: Public Archives of Canada.
HONEY, Samuel Lewis   149
Photo: Public Archives of Canada.
HORNELL, David Ernest   185
Photo: Public Archives of Canada.
HUTCHESON, Bellenden Seymour   139
Times History of the War, vol. xix, internal quotations from the *London Gazette*, December 14, 1918.
Illustration: *War Illustrated Album de Luxe*, vol. v.
KAEBLE, Joseph   105
KERR, George Fraser   145
Times History of the War, vol. xix. The quote is from *The London Gazette*, January 6, 1919.
Photo: Public Archives of Canada.
KERR, John Chipman   43
Thirty Canadian V.Cs., London, Canadian War Records Office, n.d.
Illustration: *The Sphere*, April 6, 1918.
KINROSS, Cecil John   85
Photo: Public Archives of Canada.
KNIGHT, Arthur George   133
Photo: Public Archives of Canada.
KONOWAL, Filip   71
Thirty Canadian V.Cs., London, Canadian War Records Office, n.d.

LEARMONTH, Okill Massey   67
W. W. Murray, *The History of the 2nd Canadian Battalion (Eastern Ontario Regiment)*, Ottawa, Regimental Association, Association, 1947.
LYALL, Graham Thomson   147
Photo: Public Archives of Canada.
MacDOWELL, Thain Wendell   49
Thirty Canadian V.Cs., London, Canadian War Records Office, n.d.
MacGREGOR, John   153
Times History of the War, vol. xix. The quote is from the *London Gazette*, January 6, 1919.
Photo: Public Archives of Canada.
MacKENZIE, Hugh   81
Thirty Canadian V.Cs., London, Canadian War Records Office, n.d.
Illustration: *War Illustrated Album de Luxe*, vol. ix.
MAHONY, John Keefer   181
G. W. L. Nicholson, *The Canadians in Italy*, Ottawa, Queen's Printer, 1956.
Photo: Public Archives of Canada.
McKEAN, George Burdon   101
R. C. Fetherstonhaugh, *The Royal Montreal Regiment, 14th Battalion, C.E.F., 1914-1925*, Montreal, Regimental Association, 1927.
McLEOD, Alan Arnett   97
A copy of McLeod's letter, April 8th, 1918, is held by the Canadian War Museum.
J. N. Harris, *Knights of the Air*, Toronto, Macmillan Co. of Canada, 1963.
Illustration: From *Knights of the Air*. By permission of The Macmillan Company of Canada Limited.

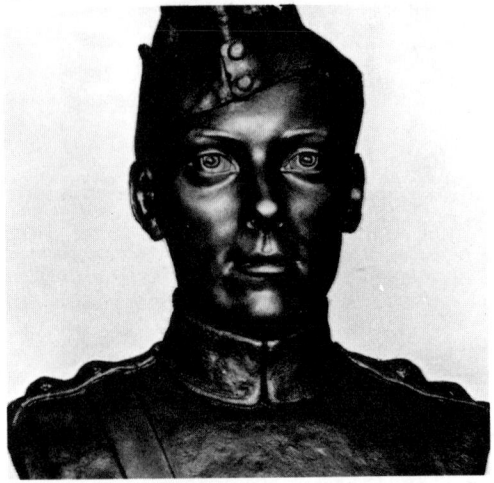

MERRIFIELD, William 155
  Times History of the War, vol. xix. The quotes are from the *London Gazette*, January 6, 1919.
  Photo: Public Archives of Canada.
MERRITT, Charles Cecil Ingersoll 171
METCALF, William Henry 135
  H. M. Urquhart, *The History of the 16th Battalion (The Canadian Scottish), C.E.F.*, Toronto, Macmillan, 1932.
  Illustration: *Times History of the War*, vol. xix.

MILNE, William Johnstone 51
  H. M. Urquhart, *The History of the 16th Battalion (The Canadian Scottish), C.E.F.*, Toronto, Macmillan, 1932.
  Photo: Public Archives of Canada.

MINER, Harry Garnet Bedford 111
  D. J. Goodspeed, *Battle Royal, A History of the Royal Regiment of Canada, 1862-1962*, Toronto, Regimental Association, 1962.
  Illustration: *War Illustrated Album de Luxe*, vol. ix.
MITCHELL, Coulson Norman 157
  A. J. Kerry and W. A. McDill, *The History of the Corps of Royal Canadian Engineers*, vol. 1, Ottawa, Military Engineers Association, 1962.
MULLIN, George Harry 83
  Ralph Hodder-Williams, *Princess Patricia's Canadian Light Infantry, 1914-1919*, Edmonton, Regimental Association, 1968, citing the *London Gazette*.
  Illustration: *War Illustrated Album de Luxe*, vol. ix.
MYNARSKI, Andrew Charles 183
NICKERSON, William Henry Snyder 222
NUNNEY, Claude Joseph Patrick 131
  Times History of the War, vol. xix. The internal quotation is from the *London Gazette*, December 14, 1918.
  Photo: Public Archives of Canada.
O'HEA, Timothy 222
O'KELLY, Christopher Patrick John 79
  G. O'M. Creagh and E. M. Humphris, *The Victoria Cross*, vol. I. of *The V.C. and D.S.O.*, London, Standard Art Book Co., n.d.
  Photo: Public Archives of Canada.
O'LEARY, Michael 29
  G. O'M. Creagh and E. M. Humphris, *The Victoria Cross*, vol. I. of *The V. C. and D.S.O.*, London, Standard Art Book Co., n.d.
  Photos: *The Sphere*, July 3rd, 1915.
O'ROURKE, Michael James 63
  T. V. Scudamore, *A Short History of the 7th Battalion, C.E.F.*, Vancouver, Regimental Association, 1930.
OSBORN, John Robert 169
  Photo: Public Archives of Canada.
PATTISON, John George 55
  Thirty Canadian V.Cs., London, Canadian War Records Office, n.d.
  Illustration: *The Sphere*, January 20th, 1917.
PATTON, John MacMillan Stevenson 205
  Kerry and McDill, *History of the Corps of Royal Canadian Engineers*, vol. II, Ottawa, Military Engineers Association, 1966.
  Photo: Directorate of History, Canadian Forces Headquarters.
PEARKES, George Randolph 87
  Photo: Public Archives of Canada.
PEARSON, John 222
PECK, Cyrus Wesley 137
  H. M. Urquhart, *The History of the 16th Battalion (The*

Canadian Scottish), C.E.F., Toronto, Macmillan, 1932.
  Photo: Public Archives of Canada.
PETERS, Frederick Thornton 175
  Photo: Courtesy, F. H. P. Dewdney.
RAYFIELD, Walter Leigh 143
  T. V. Scudamore, *A Short History of the 7th Battalion,
  C.E.F.*, Vancouver, Regimental Association, 1930.
  Photo: Public Archives of Canada.
READE, Herbert Taylor 9
  "Canada's Second Victoria Cross," by "Infantryman,"
  The Legionary, September-October, 1932.
  Illustration: From a newspaper photo in the Public
  Archives of Canada.
RENNIE, John 215
  Photo: Public Archives of Canada.
RICHARDSON, Arthur Herbert Lindsay 19
  T. G. Marquis, *Canada's Sons on Kopje and Veldt*, Toronto,
  The Canada's Son's Publishing Co., 1900.
  Photo from J. C. Ridpath, *The Story of South Africa*,
  Guelph, World Publishing Co., 1902.
RICHARDSON, George 222
RICHARDSON, James Cleland 45
  H. M. Urquhart, *The History of the 16th Battalion (The
  Canadian Scottish), C.E.F.*, Toronto, Macmillan, 1932.
  Photo: Public Archives of Canada.
RICKETTS, Thomas 161
  G. W. L. Nicholson, *The Fighting Newfoundlander*,
  St. John's, Government of Newfoundland, 1964.
  Photo: Public Archives of Canada.
ROBERTSON, James Peter 91
  Thirty Canadian V.Cs., London, Canadian War Records
  Office, n.d.
  Photo: Public Archives of Canada.
ROBSON, Henry Howey 223
ROSS, Arthur Dwight 217
  T. Coughlin, *The Dangerous Sky*, Toronto, Ryerson,
  1968.
  Photo: Public Archives of Canada.
RUTHERFORD, Charles Smith 127
  Times History of the War, vol. xviii. Internal quotations
  are from the *London Gazette*, November 15, 1918.
  Photo: *Times History of the War*, vol. xviii.
RYDER, Robert 224
SCRIMGER, Francis Alexander Caron 37
  Thirty Canadian V.Cs., London, Canadian War Records
  Office, n.d.
  Illustration: *Times History of the War*, vol. vii.
SHANKLAND, Robert 77
  Photo: *The Sphere*, February 23rd, 1918.
SIFTON, Ellis Wellwood 53
  Thirty Canadian V.Cs., London, Canadian War Records
  Office, n.d.
  Photo: Public Archives of Canada.
SMITH, Ernest Alvia 191
  G. W. L. Nicholson, *The Canadians in Italy*, Ottawa,
  Queen's Printer, 1956.
  Photo: Public Archives of Canada.
SPALL, Robert 125
  Ralph Hodder-Williams, *Princess Patricia's Canadian
  Light Infantry, 1914-1919*, Edmonton, Regimental
  Association, 1968.
  Photo: Manitoba Department of Education.
SPOONER, Kenneth Gerald 213
  Photo: Public Archives of Canada.
STRACHAN, Harcus 93
  G. O'M. Creagh and E. M. Humphris, *The Victoria Cross*,
  vol. I. of *The V. C. and D.S.O.*, London, Standard Art
  Book Co., n.d.
  Photo: Public Archives of Canada.
STUART, Ronald Neil 224
TAIT, James Edward 121
  Illustration: *War Illustrated Album de Luxe*, vol. ix.
TILSTON, Frederick Albert 195
  Cliff Bowering, "This was the Hochwald," *The Legionary*,
  March, 1955.
  Photo: Public Archives of Canada.
TOMBS, Joseph 223
TOPHAM, Frederick Albert 197
  C. P. Stacey, *The Victory Campaign*, Ottawa, Queen's
  Printer, 1969.
  Photo: Public Archives of Canada.
TRAIN, Charles William 224
TRIQUET, Paul 177
  Photo: Public Archives of Canada.
TURNER, Richard Ernest William 23
  Eyewitness, Trooper A. E. Hilder, R.C.D., from Turner
  Papers, Canadian War Museum.
  Photo: from Turner Papers, Canadian War Museum.
WILKINSON, Thomas Orde Lawder 224
YOUNG, John Francis 141
  Photo: J. M. Miller, *The People's War Book*, Toronto,
  Imperial Publishing Co., 1919.
ZENGEL, Raphael Louis 115
  Photo: Manitoba Department of Education.

Photos and Illustrations on Theme Pages:

Page 3: Army Museums Ogilby Trust (London)
Page 7: National Army Museum
Page 17: From H. W. Wilson, *After Pretoria; The Guerilla War*, Vol.
       iv., London, The Amalgamated Press, 1902.